Altars Over Thrones

How a Revival of the Altar Changes the World

John Hammer

Copyright © 2025 by John Hammer

All Scripture quotations, unless otherwise indicated, are taken from the Holy Bible, New International Version®, NIV®. Copyright ©1973, 1978, 1984, 2011 by Biblica, Inc.™ Used by permission of Zondervan. All rights reserved worldwide. www.zondervan.com The "NIV" and "New International Version" are trademarks registered in the United States Patent and Trademark Office by Biblica, Inc.™

Scriptures marked NKJV is taken from the New King James Version®. Copyright © 1982 by Thomas Nelson. Used by permission. All rights reserved.

All rights reserved.

No part of this book may be reproduced in any form or by any electronic or mechanical means, including information storage and retrieval systems, without written permission from the author, except for the use of brief quotations in a book review.

Contents

Praise for Altars Over Thrones	v
Acknowledgments	xi
Foreword	xv
Introduction	xxiii
1. The Case for Altars Over Thrones	1
2. The Altars in the Old Testament	11
3. The Altars of the New Testament	23
4. Restoring the Altar of the Heart	37
5. Restoring the Family Altar	53
6. Restoring the Church Altar	63
7. The Altar of the Region	79
8. How do we Really Change the World?	89
9. True Prophets and the Altar	103
10. Altars Gone Wrong	111
11. Obedience over Sacrifice	119
12. Priests at Altars or Sages on Stages	127
13. The Glorious Invitation to Revival	139
Appendix	151
Also by John Hammer	153
Contact	155
About the Author	157

Praise for Altars Over Thrones

Is there something broken in your life that you'd like to fix, but don't know how? After finishing my Doctoral degree in April 2024, the Holy Spirit whispered to me and said, "Leif, slow down enough so you can catch up with God."
I received a calling, how to repair, restore and rebuild Holy Altars in my life. My friend John Hammer has given us a gift of greatest value.
Altars over Thrones is a Now word and prophetic invitation for all who want to live an unshakable life in a shakable world. The fire on the Altar will burn brightly without burning out when intimacy with Jesus becomes your priority. This is a breath of clean and clarifying air.

Dr. Leif Hetland
Author of *The Love Awakening*

There has been an ongoing debate about what truly brings lasting transformation. Depending on whom you ask, the answers vary and often go beyond the average believer's pay grade.
Many times, we are offered quick-fix spiritual snake oil strategies, trendy techniques, or pedestrian political power plays. But there remains a

higher way. *Altars Over Thrones* settles the issue and calls the Church back to the timeless path of surrender and sacrifice.

John Hammer provides a prophetic answer—one that strikes a chord with a revelation blazing with an eternal flame. I believe this book will become an instant classic, standing the test of time and revolutionizing its readers. Prepare to be encountered and transformed. I highly recommend this book.

Sean Smith
@revseansmith
author of *Prophetic Evangelism* and *I Am Your Sign*
Co-Host of *Keep It 100 Podcast with Sean and Christa*
www.seanandchristasmith.com

Altars over Thrones is a powerful and timely call to restore our faith in the altar—the place of prayer, sacrifice, and divine encounter—over the pursuit of earthly power and influence. With deep biblical insight and personal conviction, Pastor John Hammer challenges us to shift our hope from political thrones to the transformative presence of God. His reflections on Elijah, the early church, and the supremacy of Christ as the Lamb enthroned are both convicting and inspiring. I love John's heart for revival, his unwavering commitment to truth, and his passion for seeing God's people return to a place of surrendered worship. This book will stir your spirit and renew your vision for what truly changes the world.

Meesh Fomenko
Be Moved
bemoved.org

I highly recommend *Altars over Thrones* to every believer who desires to see true revival in our time. This book carries a timely and powerful message—one that calls the church back to the altar of God, where real transformation happens.

Pastor John Hammer masterfully weaves biblical truth, historical examples, and personal revelation, showing that the greatest moves of God have never come through political power, status, or human effort, but through prayer, sacrifice, and surrender at the altar. Using the story of Elijah and the prophets of Baal, he reminds us that the fire of God falls where there is an altar—not on earthly thrones, but on surrendered lives.

This book is a must-read for pastors, intercessors, and all believers longing to see God move in their churches, communities, and nations. It will deepen your faith, ignite your passion for prayer, and challenge you to rebuild the altars in your life. If you are serious about revival, *Altars over Thrones* will equip and inspire you to take your place in God's plan. I strongly urge every Christian to read this book. It is a prophetic call to action—one that we cannot afford to ignore.

Dr. Fernando Cabrera
Lead Pastor of *New Life Church*
Author of *Prayer Champion*
Former NYC Councilman and Senior Advisor to the Mayor of NYC
Ranked 7th Most Influential Religious Leader in NYC by City & State

John Hammer has written, *Altars Over Thrones: How a Revival of the Altar Changes the World*, I believe the Lord has laid this message on John's heart because it is for the time we are living in now. He shares the Old Testament stories like Elijah and the prophets and kings. He gleans truth from the Bible about how important it is to build altars in our lives. The book is really a cry for us to come back to the altar in the church, our personal life and our family. I love the section on the History Makers who had an altar of prayer and changed history. Let's be stirred to pray at the altar and make history again to glorify Jesus. Read it and apply it. The Altar's open! God will change your life.

Dr. Dan C. Hammer
Senior Apostolic Leader, *Sonrise Christian Center*
Seattle Bible College President
Lead Elder, *Fellowship of Christian Assemblies*

In recent days I have heard this phrase, "Will you build Me an altar?" A place of consecration to God, but equally a place of confrontation to the enemy. This is a time to bow and acknowledge the greatness of God and then place our desires for recognition on this altar. Too many have pursued a name for themselves, building thrones and empires of false status. In this book, John carefully unpacks these tensions of power and helps us understand the right heart attitudes of the Kingdom.
So, will you build your God an altar?

Rachel Hickson
Heartcry for Change, Oxford, UK

In *Altars Over Thrones*, John Hammer issues a prophetic call to the church in America—a call to return to the place of encounter with God, intercession for His purposes, and surrender to His lordship. He exposes the subtle yet dangerous shift that has taken place in the church, where many have exchanged trust in the power of God's presence for confidence in political influence and human strategy. This book is not a rejection of cultural engagement, but a recalibration—a summons to prioritize the altar over the throne. If you long to see revival in the church and awakening in our nation, start here. This book will stir your heart, challenge your assumptions, and call you back to the place where true power is found.

Adam Narciso
YWAM Fire & Fragrance Nashville, TN

In his book *Altars over Thrones,* Pastor John Hammer unashamedly calls the church back to wholehearted devotion to the Lord in every area of our lives. This book carries incredible insights that will encourage, challenge and provoke you toward a love for the Lord and His people like you once had or perhaps never had before. If you take this book seriously, you can certainly expect fruit in your personal life and even your ministry as well.

Ben Dixon
Lead Pastor - *Northwest Church*
Author of *Hearing God* and *Prophesy*

Acknowledgments

Thank you first of all to my Lord and Savior Jesus Christ for loving me and laying down Your life on the altar to redeem me. Thank You for Your presence and grace in my life.

Grace, thank you for being the best wife a guy could ask for. You are a constant encouragement to me in my writing. Thank you for the time you let me have to invest in books like this. Thank you for being my best friend and prayer partner. I love you!

Hailey, Emma, Justus and Addi, you, my children, are so amazing and so fun. I love to see the way that you have all grown in your relationship with God. Thanks for making being a dad so great. I love how we meet with God as a family.

Carolyn, this book wouldn't have come together so well without your editing, layout and consultation. Thank you once again!

Jason, you are a man of many talents and excellent at several things! Thank you for doing the cover design once again.

Kevin, I love you my friend and I'm thankful for your art and tech skills to capture the essence of the Lamb of God who is slain, risen and forever exalted. I really love the cover art, thank you!

Sonrise Christian Center, you guys are an amazing church family. Thank you to the Elders, Staff, Deacons, intercessors and people who pray for us and support us in the call of God on our lives. We are living out much of this book together and by God's grace may we fully do so for His glory.

Bishop Joe, you have been such a blessing in this process, to not only write the foreword, open doors for this message, but ultimately to help steward the environment that this book was birthed in. Thank you for your leadership and support through *Christ Covenant Coalition* and for caring so well for Grace and I.

I dedicate this book to my Dad and Mom who lived their lives at the altar of prayer. Thank you for your faithful example of loving Jesus in the secret place and obeying Him no matter what it cost you. You have paved the way for the next generations to continue in the faith and meet God at the altar.

Foreword

I have rarely been so excited about the concepts presented in a new book! I am especially delighted that this book was written by an impressive young pastor I am in covenant with.

John Hammer is on to something in this work that is so important - I believe every pastor and serious Christ follower should prioritize reading this book *Altars Over Thrones*.

In the tapestry of human history, altars have stood as profound symbols of communion between the divine and the mortal. These sacred spaces, where heaven meets earth, have been central to spiritual practices across cultures and epochs. In the Christian tradition, the altar embodies the essence of sacrifice, worship, and divine presence. This book delves into the multifaceted significance of altars, exploring their roles in personal devotion, family unity, ecclesiastical worship, and societal transformation.

In recent years, a concerning trend has emerged within segments of the Evangelical church: a shift towards prioritizing political engagement over the foundational practices of prayer, obedience, and sacrificial living. This shift suggests a belief that civic leadership and political activism are the primary catalysts for national transformation. However, this perspective overlooks the profound biblical truth that true and lasting change originates from the altar—a place of intimate communion with God—rather than the throne of political power.

The Supremacy of the Altar Over Political Thrones

Throughout biblical narratives, altars have often been depicted as instruments of divine authority, superseding earthly powers. The patriarchs—Abraham, Isaac, and Jacob—constructed altars to honor their encounters with God, signifying allegiance to a higher sovereignty than that of mortal kings. These altars served as tangible affirmations that divine authority reigns supreme over human governance. In contemporary times, this principle challenges believers to prioritize divine directives over political ideologies, recognizing that true justice and righteousness emanate from adherence to God's will. Scripture consistently emphasizes that our battles are not merely against earthly entities, but against spiritual forces that influence the physical realm. The Apostle Paul, in Ephesians 6:12, reminds us that our struggle is "not against flesh and blood, but against... the spiritual forces of evil in the heavenly realms." This underscores the necessity of engaging in spiritual warfare through prayer and obedience, rather than relying solely on political mechanisms.

Jesus Himself declared, "My kingdom is not of this world" (John 18:36), indicating that the advancement of God's kingdom is not contingent upon earthly political structures. The early church exemplified this truth; despite facing severe persecution from governing authorities, they did not resort to political rebellion. Instead, they devoted themselves to prayer, teaching, and communal living, resulting in a transformative impact on society that political power alone could never achieve. While political engagement is a facet of societal influence, it must never supersede the primacy of the altar. Elevating political activism above spiritual disciplines can lead to a form of idolatry, where trust is placed in human institutions rather than in God's sovereign power. This misalignment can result in division within the church, as political allegiances overshadow the unifying mission of the gospel.

I agree with John Hammer when he says that when the church

neglects prayer in favor of political engagement, it forfeits the divine authority granted by God. Without the foundation of prayer and obedience, political efforts become futile, lacking the spiritual potency required to effect genuine transformation. Therefore, the church must guard against the temptation to prioritize political thrones over the sacred altar of communion with God.

In essence, the altar represents a life wholly surrendered to God—a life marked by prayer, obedience, and sacrificial love. It is from this place of humility and devotion that true transformation flows, as Christ followers influence every sphere of society.

Erecting Family and Personal Altars

The family unit, as the foundational cell of society, thrives when centered around collective worship and prayer. Establishing a family altar—a dedicated space for communal prayer, Scripture reading, and spiritual discourse—fosters unity and spiritual growth. This practice, rooted in biblical tradition, transforms households into sanctuaries of faith, where members collectively seek divine guidance and strength. In an era marked by fragmented relationships and relentless distractions, the family altar serves as a bastion of spiritual resilience and cohesion. Hence, the concept of the altar extends beyond corporate worship into the personal and familial spheres. In the Old Testament, patriarchs, like Abraham, built altars as tangible expressions of their commitment and obedience to God (Genesis 12:7). These personal altars were places of encounter, sacrifice, and covenant. In our contemporary context, establishing a personal altar signifies dedicating time and space for daily communion with God, fostering a lifestyle marked by continual surrender and alignment with His will.

Thus, the family altar serves as a cornerstone for spiritual growth within the household. Regular times of family prayer, worship, and Scripture reading cultivate an environment where faith is nurtured, and members are encouraged to live out their beliefs authentically. This practice not only strengthens familial bonds but also establishes a legacy of faith that can influence generations to come.

Christ's Altar of Sacrifice and Obedience

Central to the Christian faith is the altar of Christ's sacrifice on the cross. This ultimate act of obedience and selflessness serves as the foundation for our redemption and exemplifies the power of sacrificial love. Through His death and resurrection, Jesus triumphed over all earthly powers and authorities, disarming them and making a public spectacle of them (Colossians 2:15). This victory underscores that true authority and transformation are achieved through obedience to God and self-sacrifice, rather than through political dominance.

In Revelation 5, the imagery of the Lamb who was slain standing at the center of the throne portrays the ongoing reign of Christ over all creation. This vision reinforces that Christ's sacrificial act continues to hold supremacy over all earthly powers, and it is through aligning ourselves with His example of obedience and sacrifice that we participate in His redemptive mission for the world. The Enduring Reign of Christ's Altar in Revelation.

In light of this, we see that the Book of Revelation illustrates how the unseen realm of heaven exerts the perpetual sovereignty of Christ over creation. The Lamb who was slain is depicted as worthy to open the scroll, signifying His ultimate authority and dominion. This celestial altar serves as a testament to the enduring reign of Christ, assuring believers that despite temporal challenges, divine providence orchestrates the course of history. It is a source of hope and encouragement, affirming that faithfulness will culminate in eternal communion with the Divine.

Consequently, the crucifixion of Jesus Christ stands as the paramount altar of sacrifice, where divine love confronted and conquered the powers of the world. On the cross, Christ dismantled the dominion of sin and death, triumphing over earthly authorities and spiritual adversaries. This monumental event underscores that ultimate victory and authority belong to God, rendering all earthly thrones subordinate to His reign. Believers are thus reminded that their allegiance is to a kingdom not of this world, one established through the sacrificial act of the Savior.

Reclaiming the Church Altar

Within the church setting, there is a growing need to reclaim the significance of the altar—not merely as a physical space for prayer but as the epicenter of worship, preaching, and communal life. The altar symbolizes a place of transformation, where believers collectively offer themselves in service and devotion to God. Preaching and worship should emanate from this place of sacrifice, leading the congregation into a deeper commitment to live out their faith authentically.

Moreover, the church is called to be a "house of prayer for all nations" (Isaiah 56:7). Corporate prayer gatherings are essential for seeking God's guidance, interceding for communities, and fostering unity among believers. These gatherings serve as collective altars where the church humbles itself, seeks God's face, and turns from wicked ways, trusting in His promise to heal the land (2 Chronicles 7:14). The collective assembly of believers in corporate prayer wields transformative potential. The church altar, as a focal point for communal intercession, embodies the unity and power of the body of Christ. Regular gatherings for prayer cultivate a sense of shared purpose and dependence on divine intervention. This practice not only strengthens the faith community, but also serves as a conduit for spiritual awakening and societal impact, as collective supplication aligns the church with God's redemptive mission.

The Personal Altar of Sacrifice

Beyond physical structures, the concept of the altar extends to the personal realm, where individuals offer themselves as living sacrifices. The Apostle Paul exhorts believers in Romans 12:1 to present their bodies as "a living sacrifice, holy and pleasing to God." This personal altar signifies a daily commitment to surrender one's desires, ambitions, and will to the divine purpose. It is a call to embody the sacrificial love demonstrated by Christ, leading a life marked by humility, service, and unwavering devotion. Embracing the altar's significance entails adopting a cross-shaped (cruciform) life, mirroring the sacrificial path of Christ. This lifestyle is characterized by self-denial, compassion, and a steadfast commitment to God's will. It challenges believers to navigate the complexities of life with a posture of humility and love, bearing witness to the transformative power of the Gospel. In essence, living a cross-shaped life is an embodiment of the principles symbolized by the altar: sacrifice, devotion, and divine communion.

Establishing City and Regional Altars

Beyond the personal, family and local church altar, there is a profound need for community or city altars. These are collaborative efforts where churches across denominations come together in unified prayer and worship, interceding for societal transformation. Such unity reflects the heart of Jesus' prayer in John 17:21, "that all of them may be one... so that the world may believe." When the body of Christ stands united at the altar, it becomes a powerful catalyst for change, impacting social structures, cultural norms, and community values.

In our contemporary society, the challenges we face—rising crime rates, social fragmentation, and moral decay—underscore the urgent need for collective spiritual intervention. The concept of a "city altar" emerges as a powerful response to these issues, representing a unified platform where churches and pastors collaborate in prayer and action to transform their communities.

A city altar is more than a physical space; it symbolizes the collective commitment of the Christian community to seek divine guidance and effect positive change. By coming together in unity, churches can address societal issues more effectively than they could in isolation. This collaborative approach fosters a sense of shared responsibility and harnesses the diverse strengths of various congregations.

Establishing a city altar involves regular interdenominational gatherings focused on prayer, worship, and strategic planning to tackle community issues. Such unity not only amplifies the church's voice in public discourse but also exemplifies the teachings of Christ regarding love, unity, and service.

In essence, the creation of a city altar empowers the Christian community to collectively embody their faith, leading to profound and lasting transformation within their region.

John Hammer eloquently expounds on all of the above and much more! I'm so proud of him! My prayer is that this book will help catalyze altars being built in every facet of society so that the Lordship of Christ will be magnified to all!

Bishop Joseph Mattera
Mattera Ministries International
Christ Covenant Coalition

Introduction

Why Write Altars over Thrones?

I first wrote an outline for this book in September of 2023. I felt a stir to write on this topic after some observations I heard about the Biblical story of Elijah, and also after some preaching I did on Elijah's showdown with the prophets of Baal in 1 Kings. This phrase, *Altars over Thrones*, gripped me as I meditated on the Scriptures and thought about it as a greater meta-narrative throughout the Bible.

I have a list of books I would like to write, but obviously can't write all of them at once. So this outline just sat in one of my digital files alongside other book ideas for a later day.

In early October 2024, I was at a leadership retreat with Christ Covenant Coalition, convened by Bishop Joseph Mattera who has been a mentor and like a spiritual father to my wife Grace and I. During our retreat, different ministers were assigned a portion of Psalm 23 to teach from throughout the days we gathered.

On the second day, a move of the Holy Spirit interrupted our schedule. We all came to the altar, where we gathered during a powerful time of prayer.

As Grace and I prayed together, we felt the Holy Spirit come upon us. It was like a renewal of an impartation we had two years earlier that shifted the course of our church and ministry. I sat there in God's presence and repented, continuing to seek the Lord. I felt an urgency that as leaders in the church, we needed to repent of our exalting of thrones over altars.

The ministry has become obsessed with power, prestige, and popularity too often, and some who we considered great leaders have fallen. Our elections have been causing division and fear on the one hand, and great hope of a national revival on the other if the "right candidate wins."

As this was stirring in my heart, I was reminded of Elijah and the idea of *Altars over Thrones*.

Right after this happened, Bishop Joe got up and said something to the effect that God is doing something right now in this season concerning Elijah and the restoring of altars. He invited me up, and I shared what had been stirring in my spirit.

As I prayed, I was so overwhelmed by the power of God that I could barely stand. It was almost difficult to breathe. There was such a sense of God's presence.

I felt marked by God in that encounter.

I felt a sense that *now* is the time for the message of *Altars over Thrones*.

Is it the cross or the sword that has most radically shaped the world?

I went back to my seat and opened my note files to see the outline I had started almost a year before, and I realized that God is alerting me, and not only me, but the church in America, to restore our faith in the power of the altar once again.

From my observation, the people of God have lost faith in the power of altars and are mesmerized by the power of thrones.

Our hopes and fears for the future of our ministries, churches, cities and nation are overly tied to *who* occupies human thrones of politics, celebrity and influence. In the United States of America, we face a crisis every four years known as a presidential election. With every election and campaigning season, I now hear people say, "This is surely the most important election of our lifetime." Many are persuaded that if we can only get the right person in office, we will finally have revival and awakening in our great nation once again.

Many believers are now convinced that if we could just get more Christians voting and involved in politics, we could "save our nation." If we just produce better programs, gain more followers, have more money or power, we could really turn things around.

While I believe that Christians should be involved politically by voting, working in government and by running for office, I believe we have things out of order and have put more faith in our activism and participation in earthly things by thrones, than in the heavenly power we have been given through altars.

I would like to assure you that this book is not altars instead of thrones, it's *Altars over Thrones*. We should not ignore the importance of thrones, but interact with them from the proper place of faith and perspective.

I also want to assure you that I'm not implying our altars are superior to God's throne. God reigns over all. Earthly altars are connected to heaven's altar and heaven's throne. God has elevated the lowly altar because of His Son's sacrifice on it.

God sized problems take God size solutions. God shaped holes in the church, in cities and in society cannot be filled by human effort. It's going to take God to solve and heal the problems facing our nation.

Why do we think that the leadership of the Whitehouse is more powerful than the leadership of God's house?

Why do we think whoever has the most popularity or earthly power makes the biggest difference?

Have we replaced our conviction that the apostle Paul has more to say to us than Caesar? Have we lost faith in the suffering Savior and put our hope in another Pilate or Herod? Is it the cross or the sword that has most radically shaped the world?

Forget even thinking about politics and culture for a moment.

Have we lost faith in the power of sacrifice, humility, confession, and repentance? Have we lost faith in the conviction that God meets with us and answers us at altars?

May God recover our faith in the power and authority we have when we build altars unto Him, the Almighty, who is seated on heaven's throne as the Lamb slain on the altar for us.

It's time for a holy visitation and a return to the altar so that we don't miss anything that heaven intends to pour out in this hour.

I've never felt more unqualified to write on a subject. I've never felt more of a stirring and sense of God's presence as I write. I present this work as an offering, not of perfection but as something that I pray honors the Lord and moves hearts to get before the Lord's altar in faith for another great awakening.

Karl Barth once said, "To clasp the hands in prayer is the beginning of an uprising against the disorder of the world."[1] My hope is that after reading this book you will join me at the altar with hands clasped in prayer fully persuaded that this is how we change the world.

---

1. https://www.goodreads.com/quotes/1601-to-clasp-the-hands-in-prayer-is-the-beginning-of

Chapter 1

The Case for Altars Over Thrones

In 2022, I was watching an episode of the *Dr. Jordan B. Peterson Podcast* on YouTube[1]. He had a discussion with a guest named Vishal Mangalwadi. Mangalwadi is a Christian and a philosopher from India who has written books on the power of the Bible to shape the world. I've seen dozens of Dr. Peterson's podcasts over the years, but this episode in particular, with the stories and insights of Mangalwadi, gripped me and prompted me to explore further the Biblical revelation of the power of altars over thrones.

Mangalwadi shares about his upbringing in India. He went through different periods in his life where he put his faith in God, and a time in his life where he abandoned his Christian faith to become a seeker of religious truth through Buddhist thought and study. He eventually felt the truth was unknowable, but he wanted to test this idea by studying various philosophies and beliefs. His sister finally convinced him to read the Bible. He was against this idea because he felt they were mere childish stories. But she persuaded him to read the Bible not as he did as a child but as a philosopher.

---

1. Youtube video with Mangdawali and Peterson https://youtu.be/QvESPeFWLHw?si=Dgenz9UHt3OS9PD8

When he reached the historical books of the Kings and Chronicles, he was almost ready to give up on the whole of the Bible. He found himself bored and frustrated trying to make sense of the Biblical text. When he got to the story of a widow and Elijah in the North of Israel, God got his attention. He started to see the concept of revelation and that truth could be communicated through the word of God. Elijah and the prophets had a power in their words that superseded the will and words of King Ahab. This, along with his continued reading of the effect of Jesus' and Paul's lives in the New Testament led him to a place of faith in Christ that was revealed to Him by God through the Scriptures.

As he shared, I was so moved by this truth that on the one hand, it makes sense that kings are the highest authority in the land and should be able to do whatever they want. However, there is a higher authority to which even they are beholden. The king has ascended to an earthly throne, but there is a limit to ascent. There is a lid that limits the heights of what a king can choose to do and no matter what, even he cannot escape the consequences of his choices.

There is a price to pay to truly walk with God in every generation.

Can't a king create a new law if he wants to do whatever is in his heart, making that thing now acceptable because he is the highest authority in the land?

No.

Why?

Because there is a law and a throne that exists, even kings and rulers must honor, or they will face judgement. Various Biblical accounts make this abundantly clear.

Let's look at two stories from the prophet Elijah's life.

The Showdown

In 1 Kings 18, Elijah had a showdown with the prophets of Baal, a few years after he prophesied it would not rain in Israel for 3 years until he said so. King Ahab and Queen Jezebel had aligned the people of God with the false god Baal; Baal means owner, lord, husband, or master.

Baal was a Canaanite god who, according to them, was in charge of the weather. And now Elijah the prophet shows up and exposes the impotence of Baal by proclaiming that the One true God would not allow it to rain to a people who were supposedly serving the god who sent the rain.

Ahab was angry at Elijah and the true prophets of the Lord, because a great famine had resulted from those few years without rain.

With Elijah's agreement, Obadiah—a prophet in hiding who harbored a hundred others out of fear for their lives—brought Elijah before King Ahab. King Ahab's first words to Elijah when he laid eyes on him were, "Is that you, you troubler of Israel?"[2]

Elijah wasn't a hero at this moment, he was a villain.

So are the heroes of the faith in the eyes of the world.

They are disruptors of the ways of this world, daring to follow God when it's not popular or when it could cost them everything.

We think of Biblical figures like Noah, Moses, Elijah and the apostles as great men of God who changed the world. But at the time of their testing and faithfulness to God, in spite of persecution, they were considered troublers, rebels, and those that were making society worse. There is a price to pay to truly walk with God in every generation.

Elijah didn't mince words. He let King Ahab know he was the true troubler of Israel, for he and his family had abandoned the Lord for Baal.

So Elijah calls for a head-to-head challenge on Mount Carmel. He tells Ahab to summon nine hundred prophets to come and meet him for this showdown; four hundred and fifty prophets of Baal and four hundred and fifty prophets of Asherah (a goddess of fertility connected to Baal).

---

2. 1 Kings 18:17

He tells the king what he is really after: the true showdown is between the Lord God and Baal.

Elijah says, "How long will you waver between two opinions, If the Lord is God, follow Him, but if Baal is God, follow Him."[3]

The tension was thick; the people, silent.

So here the people assembled at Mount Carmel to see what this contest was going to be about. You had the one true prophet of God, Elijah, versus nine hundred prophets of this false god and goddess.

But as I've often heard Graham Cooke say, "One person with God is always a majority."[4]

Elijah issues the terms: each side gets one bull to cut in pieces and place on wood to burn as a sacrifice to their god. But here is the catch: they don't get to start their own fire. Each side has to call on their deity to see who answers from heaven with fire on their sacrifice.

Elijah was going to let God be God. This is a True lesson of the altar.

Elijah says, "The god who answers by fire, he is God."[5]

The prophets of Baal and Asherah go first. They put on quite a show, calling on Baal from morning until noon. They shouted and danced. They even ended up cutting themselves with swords and spears.

Elijah even taunted them, saying, "Shout louder! Surely he is a god! Perhaps he is deep in thought, or busy, or traveling. Maybe he is sleeping and must be awakened."[6]

But there was no response from Baal.

As evening approached and it was time for the evening sacrifice,

---

3. 1 Kings 18:21
4. Graham Cooke repeated this line in several sermons I heard in the early 2000s when he preached at my church Sonrise Christian Center.
5. 1 Kings 18:24
6. 1 Kings 18:27

Elijah gathered the people around and repaired the altar of the Lord, which had been torn down. He took twelve stones for each of the twelve tribes of Israel.

But then he did something interesting. He dug a trench around the altar, and after laying the bull on some wood on the altar, he emptied four large jars of water all over the offering and the altar. He had them do this three times so that the water even filled the ditch around the altar.

Elijah wanted everyone to know that the situation was not favorable for a fire, but God doesn't need ideal circumstances. Perhaps sometimes we have it too easy and God is waiting for the moment where only He can get the glory. Sometimes He is waiting for the ditch to get a little deeper and the wood a little wetter. Elijah was going to let God be God. This is a true lesson of the altar.

Elijah prayed to the God of Abraham, Isaac, and Jacob. And as we see many times in Scripture, the fire falls on the sacrifice.

The crowd erupted, "The Lord---He is God! The Lord---He is God!"[7]

The one true God had turned the hearts of His people back through His power at the altar.

This led to mass revival and restoration. The people slayed the false prophets of Baal.

Ahab left after Elijah told him that the heavy rain was now coming after years of drought.

Elijah was waiting to pray for rain until Baal was exposed as false, so people would know where the true power lies. The throne's empty allegiance to a false god was outed on that day. The altar prevailed and Elijah began to pray.

At His fervent prayer, the rains returned, and the name of the true God was vindicated.

---

7. 1 Kings 18:39

Ahab and the Vineyard

There was another encounter that Elijah and Ahab had together that further demonstrates the case for altars over thrones.

There was a man named Naboth who had a vineyard in Jezreel and it was close to King Ahab's palace. Ahab wanted the vineyard for himself, but Naboth would not relinquish it to him. Ahab sulked in front of Jezebel, and she responded by reminding him of the power of his throne. She basically said, "Aren't you the king? And you're going to allow people to treat you this way?"

Jezebel concocts a plan and writes a story in a letter. But it's not a true story. It's a lie to set up the people against Naboth. Her evil plan works. People bring charges against Naboth that he cursed God and king.

> **The course of history has been changed more by the altar than the throne.**

So the people drag Naboth outside the city and stone him to death. Jezebel hears of his death and tells Ahab that Naboth is out of the way so he can go claim the vineyard.

The Bible says, "Then the word of the Lord came to Elijah the Tishbite: "Go down to meet Ahab king of Israel, who rules in Samaria. He is now in Naboth's vineyard, where he has gone to take possession of it. Say to him, 'This is what the Lord says: Have you not murdered a man and seized his property?' Then say to him, 'This is what the Lord says: In the place where dogs licked up Naboth's blood, dogs will lick up your blood---yes, yours!'"[8]

Elijah prophesied judgements on Ahab and Jezebel. His judgements came to pass as the word of the Lord foretold.

---

8. 1 Kings 21:18-19

Their power on the throne was limited on the earth. There was a higher law at play than even the law or will of the king. Elijah carried a power that gave him more authority than the king and queen to effect change in the earth.

The Pattern Continues

We can see this pattern repeated throughout Scripture in the Old and New Testament. The apostle Paul shakes the Roman empire with a ministry of prayer, preaching, church planting, and miracles.

When Paul and Silas are in Thessalonica, they are confronted by a mob that cries out "These who have turned the world upside down have come here too."[9]

How could a small group of apostles "turn the world upside down?"

They didn't have a military or positions of political power. But they were men of spiritual power, men who met God at the altar.

The course of history has been changed more by the altar than the throne.

Of course, Paul was only so powerful as He followed Jesus. We see this ultimately in the life of Jesus, that altars are over thrones. Jesus repeats multiple times throughout His ministry that He came to die. The resurrection was not God's emergency plan for things gone wrong against Jesus. His life was lived to become an offering for sin and to bring redemption to all mankind.

Jesus remade the world through His sacrifice. We will look at this more in a later chapter.

The Key to it All

This truth about the purpose of Christ coming into the world as a sacrifice for us on the altar is so powerful, it becomes the interpretive key for understanding all Scripture, and even the meaning of life.

Maybe that's a tall claim. But I want you to see that God's creation and actions throughout human history were founded on the reality that

---

9. Acts 17:6 NKJV

Jesus, the Son of God, would come inserted into His own creation to redeem us all through sacrifice.

> Revelation 13:8b says, *"the Lamb who was slain from the creation of the world."*

The book at the end tells us that the very beginning or foundation of the world was the Lamb slain for us. When God said, "Let there be light" in Genesis 1:3, God had already planned that He would become incarnate to rescue humanity.

The apostle Peter confirms this message in his first epistle, "He (Jesus, the Lamb) was chosen before the creation of the world, but was revealed in these last times for your sake."[10]

The whole Bible comes into focus when you understand the preeminence of Christ and how the Bible is telling one unified story that's cross-referenced over thousands of years, about the Lamb who was chosen and slain for us at the beginning of the world.

The Lamb slain on the altar for us is seated on the throne. Forever the altar is over the throne because the one from the altar is on the throne.

My parents once hosted a missionary preacher named George Stormont, who had traveled with Smith Wigglesworth earlier in his life. I only met him when I was a small child, but I never forgot the three-part sermon series my dad told me he preached.

He preached a summary of the whole Bible in three sermons through "Three Cries."

"The Cry of the Old Testament is Where is the Lamb of God?"

---

10. 1 Peter 1:20

"The Cry Between the Testaments (of John the Baptist) is Behold the Lamb of God."

"The Cry of the New Testament is Worthy is the Lamb of God."

The Bible comes alive when you realize the major movements in Scripture are preparing us to know and receive Jesus as Savior and Lord.

As soon as Adam and Eve sin, God prophesied that a Seed is coming from the woman to crush Satan. It's a prophecy about the Lamb.

We see the need for sacrifice in God preparing animal coverings for the fallen first humans. We see the Lamb's blood is needed in the Passover to escape death and the story of Exodus. We see through the law and prophets that a Lamb is coming to pay for our sins and redeem us all.

This is not only the pattern of Scripture and the life of Jesus, it is the pattern for the truth and reality of our lives. When Jesus is at the center of our lives, we become a temple, a dwelling place for God's presence, and an altar, a place that connects heaven and earth.

As Jesus walked, so are we to walk. He experienced suffering and glory and we are to share in the same suffering and glory as His followers. He remade a new humanity by conquering death in His death.

Jesus changed the world by an altar.

Jesus is reigning in heaven on the throne forever. His humiliation led to his eternal exaltation. When John the Revelator sees a great scene in heaven, he sees Jesus the slain Lamb. Revelation 5:6a says, "Then I saw a Lamb, looking as if it had been slain, standing at the center of the throne, encircled by the four living creatures and the elders."

The Lamb slain on the altar for us is seated on the throne. Forever, the altar is over the throne because the one from the altar is on the throne.

The Lamb enthroned will always bear the marks of His suffering on the altar.

We must return our faith to the power of the altar over the throne.

Chapter 2

The Altars in the Old Testament

The Bible is an incredible interconnected text with one grand narrative that tells the great story of God from Genesis to Revelation. These individual Bible stories are linked together, giving us truth and meaning as we explore these various topics; especially within the great context of this unified message about Jesus.

I want to take us through some of the great Bible characters and stories about altars throughout the Old Testament that teach us what an altar is, what they tell us about God, and what they tell us about ourselves.

Adam and Eve in Paradise

Genesis 3:21 "The Lord God made garments of skin for Adam and his wife and clothed them."

In the Garden of Eden, after the serpent deceived Adam and Eve and they ate the forbidden fruit, God pronounced a curse on the serpent and humanity. When sin entered the world through their disobedience, they experienced shame and guilt for the first time as humans.

They realized they were naked and covered themselves with fig leaves. God made them clothes as He expelled them from Paradise. We don't see an explicit reference to an altar here, but we see the truth that something would have to be sacrificed and die to cover the guilt and shame of our rebellion against God.

Cain and Abel

Genesis 4:3-5 "In the course of time Cain brought some of the fruits of the soil as an offering to the Lord. And Abel also brought an offering---fat portions from some of the firstborn of his flock. The Lord looked with favor on Abel and his offering, but on Cain and his offering he did not look with favor. So Cain was very angry, and his face was downcast."

Cain and Abel are the first children of Adam and Eve. We see here that sin corrupted the first family not only in the garden but with jealousy and hatred that resulted in murder. All this took place over a sacrifice. Again, we don't yet see the word altar appear in the Bible story, but we learn an altar principle that there are acceptable and unacceptable sacrifices we can bring before God.

Noah

Genesis 8:20-21, "Then Noah built an altar to the Lord and, taking some of all the clean animals and clean birds, he sacrificed burnt offerings on it. The LORD smelled the pleasing aroma and said in his heart: "Never again will I curse the ground because of humans, even though every inclination of the human heart is evil from childhood. And never again will I destroy all living creatures, as I have done.""

This is the first mention of the word altar in the Bible. Noah was the one righteous man God found when he saw that the rest of humanity had given themselves over to complete evil and wickedness.

God saved Noah and his family by giving him the plans to build an ark. Noah obeyed God in building the ark, and his family and animals of every kind were spared through a worldwide flood which destroyed the earth.

After about a year of total time on the ark, Noah, his family and the animals were able to exit and re-inhabit the earth. The first thing Noah did was build an altar to the Lord and offer a sacrifice. This sacrifice was a pleasing aroma to the Lord.

The altar is a place of thanksgiving for God's salvation and deliverance.

The altar is first mentioned as a place of praise.

The altar releases God's promises over us.

It's at the altar that God promises not to destroy all living creatures again.

The altar releases the joy and blessing that is in God's heart.

Abraham

> *Genesis 12:7-8, "The Lord appeared to Abram and said, "To your offspring I will give this land." So he built an altar there to the Lord, who had appeared to him. From there he went on toward the hills east of Bethel and pitched his tent, with Bethel on the west and Ai on the east. There he built an altar to the called on the name of the Lord."*

Abraham builds altars to the Lord several times in his life of following God in faith. The first time this happens is when God introduces Abraham to the Covenant He is making with Abraham and his descendants.

Abraham believed the word of the Lord that God would make a great nation out of his children and their offspring, and his response to God's Covenant promise is to build an altar.

At the altar Abraham gives himself to prayer.

Altars are a place to commemorate the things that God has spoken to us and to respond in prayer to things God reveals to us.

Abraham and Isaac

Genesis 22:9, "When they reached the place God had told him about, Abraham built an altar there and arranged the wood on it. He bound his son Isaac and laid him on the altar, on top of the wood."

Through the struggle of barrenness and infertility, Abraham and His wife Sarah finally get their promise of an heir to fulfill the covenant promise that God would make a great nation from their descendants.

But then God tells Abraham something very shocking in Genesis 22. He tells Abraham that he needs to go sacrifice his only child of promise on an altar.

Other gods in the ancient near east practiced child sacrifice. So this seems like a strange thing to do when your first promised child comes at one hundred years old. But Abraham says something powerful to his traveling companions, "We will go and worship."

As he takes Isaac up the mountain, he builds an altar and gets ready to sacrifice his son on it. The Angel of the Lord interrupts him and lets him know that he is not like the other gods. He provides a ram for a sacrifice in the bushes, and Abraham declares to God, "You are the Lord who Provides."

Altars are a place that connect earth with heaven.

We learn in this story where the first time worship is mentioned, that true worship at the altar is about obedience to God's word.

Abraham loved God more than His promise. He loved the One who orders our destiny more than his own destiny.

The altar was a test and a revelation. A test to see if he would obey out of a love for God, and a revelation that the God of the Bible provides His own sacrifice at the altar. It's a picture of Jesus taking our place on the altar.

Isaac

Genesis 26:25, "Isaac built an altar and called on the name of the Lord. There he pitched his tent, and there his servants dug a well."

Isaac continued to build altars as a place to call on God in prayer, as his father Abraham did before him. Isaac led his family in the way that was handed down to him by his family. The altar is a way to generationally pass down our faith and example of trusting God in prayer.

Jacob

Genesis 35:1, "Then God said to Jacob, "Go up to Bethel and settle there, and build an altar there to God, who appeared to you when you were fleeing from your brother Esau.""

Jacob, a patriarch of the Jewish and Christian faith, along with his father Isaac and grandfather Abraham, also builds altars to the Lord. The altar he builds in Genesis 35 is an altar of remembering and commemorating God's faithfulness to him.

It was here at Bethel that God revealed Himself to Jacob. When he was running for his life, God met Jacob and gave him a revelation about the house of God. This place is a prophetic foreshadowing of the church, Bethel, the house of God, where heaven and earth are connected. Altars are a place that connect earth with heaven.

Moses

Exodus 17:5, "Moses built an altar and called it The Lord is my Banner."

Moses leads Israel in a miraculous victory over the Amalekites. As Moses holds his staff up over his head on the hill looking at the battle between the armies, Israel wins. When he lowers his staff, they start to lose.

So Moses' companions hold up his arms and they defeat the Amalekites. Moses builds an altar to thank the Lord and declare one of His sacred names, "The Lord is my Banner."

This altar was about honor for who God is and what God does.

Exodus 20:24, "'Make an altar of earth for me and sacrifice on it your burnt offerings and fellowship offerings, your sheep and goats and your cattle. Wherever I cause my name to be honored, I will come to you and bless you."

The altar is a place of repentance, not boasting, of sacrifice, not accomplishment, and of yielding, not earning.

After leading God's people through many challenges to Mount Sinai, Moses receives the Ten Commandments from the Lord. After this incredible revelation from God, God says to Moses that wherever Moses builds an altar and makes a sacrifice to Him, He causes His name to be honored. And not only that, but in that place of honor, He will come to Moses and bless Moses.

Altars that honor the Lord bring God's presence and God's blessing.

Exodus 20:25, "If you make an altar of stones for me, do not build it with dressed stones, for you will defile it if you use a tool on it."

When Moses gets this weighty revelation about the power of altars to draw the Presence of God and the blessing of God, he gets a simple instruction that altars are not to be built with tools, nor are they to be perfect.

God does not want the altar to be a place of performance and merit, but a place of trust, worship, and surrender. The altar is a place of repentance, not boasting, of sacrifice, not accomplishment, and of yielding, not earning.

The Tabernacle

Leviticus 6:12, "The fire on the altar must be kept burning; it must not go out. Every morning the priest is to add firewood and arrange the burnt offering on the fire and burn the fat of the fellowship offerings on it."

The Tabernacle of Moses actually had two altars, an altar for burnt offerings where animals and grains were offered to the Lord for sacrifices, and an altar of incense that was for sweet aroma to the Lord. In the tabernacle of Moses, the fire on the altar was to be kept burning perpetually.

One of the jobs of the priests was to make sure the fire never goes out. We learn from the altar at the tabernacle that a priest is to always keep fire burning before the Lord. The first ministry anyone should have is to the Lord.

Leviticus 17:11, "For the life of a creature is in the blood, and I have given it to you to make atonement for yourselves on the altar; it is the blood that makes atonement for one's life."

A lamb, an ox, or a goat was brought by the people of Israel to the tabernacle to atone for their sins. God, in His mercy and grace, allowed a sacrifice to atone for the sins of His people. The altar was a place where animals were sacrificed. This was a prophetic type of how Jesus would one day give His blood for us and lay His life down for us to make atonement for our sins.

Defiled Altars

Deuteronomy 7:5, "This is what you are to do to them: Break down their altars, smash their sacred stones, cut down their Asherah poles and burn their idols in the fire."

In Deuteronomy, we learn about the evil power of altars. Usually we see in the Torah, the first five books of the Bible, the power of altars to the God of Abraham, Isaac and Jacob. But now we see that God allows for no mixture of altars. He does not tolerate altars built to Him while simultaneously allowing altars to stand to other idols. He gives these instructions to Israel that when they conquer another people, they must destroy all altars to idols and other gods.

Altars to the Lord have power to bless and release God's presence. Altars to idols release the presence of evil and defile a land spiritually. Altars are a type of portal that connect you to good or evil, to God or Satan, to Heaven or Hell.

> **Altars are a type of portal that connect you to good or evil, to God or Satan, to Heaven or Hell.**

Joshua

Joshua 8:30-31, "Then Joshua built on Mount Ebal an altar to the Lord, the God of Israel, as Moses the servant of the Lord had commanded the Israelites. He built it according to what is written in the Book of the Law of Moses—an altar of uncut stones, on which no iron tool had been used. On it they offered to the Lord burnt offerings and sacrificed fellowship offerings."

Joshua shadowed Moses through his leadership of Israel. Throughout the story of Moses leading the people of Israel through the wilderness and towards the promised land, Moses was mentoring Joshua around the presence of God. When Moses prayed, built an altar or went to seek the Lord, Joshua was by his side as much as he could be.

We see in Joshua that God uses the altar to mentor the next generation around the value and practice of ministering to the Lord.

Gideon

Judges 6:24-26, "So Gideon built an altar to the Lord there and called it The Lord Is Peace. To this day it stands in Ophrah of the Abiezrites. That same night the Lord said to him, "Take the second bull from your father's herd, the one seven years old. Tear down your father's altar to Baal and cut down the Asherah pole beside it. Then build a proper kind of altar to the Lord your God on the top of this height. Using the wood of the Asherah pole that you cut down, offer the second bull as a burnt offering."

Gideon is in hiding when God speaks to him with confirming signs that he is called to be a leader of God's people as the Lord's judge. In this place of calling and confirmation, Gideon calls this place "the Lord is Peace" and builds an altar to the Lord.

Interestingly enough, he doesn't stop there. He follows the Lord's instruction to destroy his father's altar to the false god of Baal and cut down the Asherah pole. The wood from the Asherah pole becomes fuel for the next sacrifice on the altar.

Altars can be built in the places that were once occupied by sin, compromise, and idols. Altars are this very place of redemption and even for entire families. Where once something evil was exalted by a family, now God can redeem it and use that very point of evil as a testimony for a new altar of His goodness.

King David

2 Samuel 24:25, "David built an altar to the Lord there and sacrificed burnt offerings and fellowship offerings. Then the Lord answered his prayer in behalf of the land, and the plague on Israel was stopped."

King David sinned against God by counting the people in the land without God's blessing. God judged him and he had three different consequences to choose from. He chose to let judgment go into the hands of God, believing God would be more merciful than any man. As a plague swept through Israel for this judgment, David built an altar and stopped the plague prematurely through his prayer. We learn at this altar that when we seek God in repentance and humility, He responds in mercy.

The Kings

2 Kings 21:3, "He rebuilt the high places his father Hezekiah had destroyed; he also erected to Baal and made an Asherah pole, as Ahab king of Israel had done. He bowed down to all the starry hosts and worshiped them."

King Manasseh was an evil king in Israel who built altars to false gods and idols that his father, King Hezekiah, had destroyed. We see these cycles over and over again with the Kings of Israel and Judah. Some of them, like Hezekiah, tear down idols and altars to these false gods, others like his son build them. God's blessing comes on the kings who honor His temple and altar. God's judgment comes on those who build altars to pagan gods.

Through the kings, we learn God desires our worship to Him without mixture. He alone is the only true God who deserves worship, and He will not bless our lives when we worship at other altars.

Isaiah and the Prophets

Isaiah 1:11 "The multitude of your sacrifices---what are they to me?" says the Lord. "I have more than enough of burnt offerings, of rams and the fat of fattened animals; I have no pleasure in the blood of bulls and lambs and goats."

The book of Isaiah begins with a heavy condemnation from the Lord against the people of Israel, His chosen people. He tells them He doesn't want their sacrifices anymore. The ritual sacrifices God Himself instituted in Israel had now become something God no longer desired. Israel was missing the point.

They were walking in disobedience but trying to cover their disobedience by performing these religious rituals. The altar is not a place to cover up your disobedience. God loves the altar, but not when it's misused to empower rebellion against Him.

This type of rebuke and judgment from the Lord is repeated over and over again in the prophetic books by many of the prophets.

Isaiah 6:6, "Then one of the seraphim flew to me with a live coal in his hand, which he had taken with tongs from the altar."

In Isaiah 6, when King Uzziah dies and the earthly throne is shaken, the young prophet Isaiah sees the Lord high and lifted up. He sees the beauty, majesty, and glory of the Lord.

The gospel of John tells us later that this was actually an encounter with the pre-incarnate Son of God.

In this encounter with the Lord, an angel takes a coal off the altar and touches it to the mouth of Isaiah to cleanse and commission him. We learn at this altar that our encounters with the Lord cleanse us and call us to our purpose.

There is a heavenly altar. At this altar we are made worthy by the cleansing that God provides and we are marked for commissioning by His fire, which purifies us.

Summary

In the Old Covenant, we see that the altar is a place of sacrifice. There are many lessons we learn that teach us about who God is, what He requires, and also teach us about ourselves.

Here is a summary of what we learn through the Old Testament altars. Altars are:

- a place of worship and obedience to the Lord.
- a place to thank God and remember the great things He has done.
- a place for families and God's people to worship.
- a powerful way to pass down our faith and worship to the next generation.
- a place for ministers to serve God and keep feeding the fire on it.
- dangerous and cursed if built for idols, but bring God's manifest presence and blessing when done in honor to the Lord.
- a place that can become performance driven, where we try to hide our disobedience with good outward works, but God not is not pleased with this type of sacrifice.
- a place for genuine encounters with God which are the very connection between earth and heaven.
- places of contrition and repentance.
- a place of devotion to God that brings His blessing and favor on our lives.
- a place of atonement for our sins.
- a place of God's manifest presence.
- a place of cleansing, consecration, and calling.

CHAPTER 3

THE ALTARS OF THE NEW TESTAMENT

The interconnected theme of the altar in the Old Testament is incomplete without connecting it to the New Testament. The Old Covenant altars prepared humanity for the New Covenant's Lamb of God, culminating God's plan of redemption.

JOHN THE BAPTIST

Matthew 3:3-11 "This is he who was spoken of through the prophet Isaiah: A voice of one calling in the wilderness, 'Prepare the way for the Lord, make straight paths for him.' " John's clothes were made of camel's hair, and he had a leather belt around his waist. His food was locusts and wild honey. People went out to him from Jerusalem and all Judea and the whole region of the Jordan. Confessing their sins, they were baptized by him in the Jordan River. But when he saw many of the Pharisees and Sadducees coming to where he was baptizing, he said to them: "You brood of vipers! Who warned you to flee from the coming wrath? Produce fruit in keeping with repentance. And do not think you can say to yourselves, 'We have Abraham as our father.' I tell you that out of these stones God can raise up children for Abraham. The ax is already at the root of the trees, and every tree that does not produce good fruit will be cut down and thrown into the fire. "I baptize you with water for repentance. But after me comes one who is more powerful than I, whose sandals I am not worthy to carry. He will baptize you with the Holy Spirit and fire."'

John the Baptist never refers to altars, but he is preparing the people of God to look to the final fulfillment of what altars are all about in the New Covenant. John's life and ministry shook the people of Israel, and his voice was so threatening to the political establishment of his day that King Herod had him executed.

Some might argue Herod had the upper hand and his throne prevailed over the altar in this instance, but John the Baptist went down in history as the greatest man that ever lived, according to Jesus Himself.

And what did Herod leave as a legacy? He was a cowardly and immoral king who bowed to the whims of his controlling wife.

> **Although it wasn't called this in his time, John started what is similar to modern day altar calls.**

John was a relative of Jesus, and he had a very specific commission to wrap up the Old Testament prophets and prepare the way for Jesus. He called people to repentance and authenticity. Although it wasn't called this in his time, John started what is similar to modern day altar calls. His baptisms were a time where people came forward and publicly confessed their sins at baptism. Jesus and His apostles would bring the fullness of water baptism into being, but John was there to show us the way of humility, turning from sin and living in obedience.

John 1:29 "The next day John saw Jesus coming toward him and said, "Look, the Lamb of God, who takes away the sin of the world!"

Ultimately, John did not just point to a way of authentic living and honesty, he pointed to Jesus. He is considered the greatest of all the prophets by Jesus. We have no record of him doing miracles, possessing supernatural power, having great visions or accurate predictions about the future. Yet he is considered the greatest because he pointed people to Jesus Christ, the Lamb of God who came to take away the sin of the world.

John is the exclamation point on all the other prophets. He is declaring all the other prophecies from thousands of years about the Messiah as fulfilled now in the incarnation of Jesus; the Son of God in divinity, putting on humanity.

The Lamb has arrived. The Lamb whose shadow was seen throughout the Old Testament was now here in person. John is giving voice to the reality that the altar is about to be occupied by the ultimate sacrifice to atone for the sins of humanity.

Jesus Christ

Mark 8:27-33, "Jesus and his disciples went on to the villages around Caesarea Philippi. On the way he asked them, "Who do people say I am?" They replied, "Some say John the Baptist; others say Elijah; and still others, one of the prophets." "But what about you?" he asked. "Who do you say I am?" Peter answered, "You are the Messiah." Jesus warned them not to tell anyone about him. He then began to teach them that the Son of Man must suffer many things and be rejected by the elders, the chief priests and the teachers of the law, and that he must be killed and after three days rise again. He spoke plainly about this, and Peter took him aside and began to rebuke him. But when Jesus turned and looked at his disciples, he rebuked Peter. "Get behind me, Satan!" he said. "You do not have in mind the concerns of God, but merely human concerns."

Just as Jesus was heralded as the Lamb of God who takes away the sin of the world by John the Baptist, He affirms throughout His ministry that He did indeed come to be the sacrifice for our sins.

The destiny of Jesus was the altar. Right when Peter had the revelation from God that Jesus is indeed the Son of God and the Messiah, Jesus shocked His disciples, not the least being Peter.

> **The destiny of Jesus was the altar.**

Peter goes from being affirmed that He sees Jesus clearly as the Messiah to being rebuked as satanic for not being able to see Jesus as needing to suffer. Jesus had revealed that He must suffer, be killed, and rise again. Jesus repeats this two more times in the gospel of Mark.

He came to die. He not only came to show us who God really is, teach us, perform miracles, and live among us. He came to die for us.

John 5:39-40, "You study the Scriptures diligently because you think that in them you have eternal life. These are the very Scriptures that testify about me, yet you refuse to come to me to have life."

Jesus rebuked the Jewish leaders in John 5 because they were the experts on the Scriptures, but they missed the point. Jesus wanted them, and us, to see that the Scriptures were telling a cohesive story woven across the texts.

And that cohesive story is all about Him. Jesus is the point of the Scriptures. The prophecies, the types, the shadows, the pictures and appearances of the Angel of the Lord are all about Him.

The altars of the Old Covenant are all pointing to being fulfilled in Jesus. We can be an expert on all the altars and types of theology, but if they don't bring us to Jesus, then we have missed the point. We are like experts on a treasure map, who never go to get the treasure if we know the information but don't know Christ and His life.

John 8:28, "So Jesus said, "When you have lifted up the Son of Man, then you will know that I am he and that I do nothing on my own but speak just what the Father has taught me."

Jesus said here in John 8 that He would be known by being lifted up. He is speaking about the cross.

Our God has chosen to be known by the place of sacrifice. God has eternally linked Himself to this place of execution and suffering.

Jesus is the point of the Scriptures.

The Lord of glory came to be sacrificed for us. Oh, the beauty and the irony of Jesus being lifted up. We often think of being lifted up or exalted as praising someone and giving them a place of prominence. Jesus' lifting up is being exalted on a cross.

We only truly know God by the altar. The Son of God Divine added humanity to His divinity and came to love us through suffering.

He came to love us by laying down His life on the altar for us.

And this is how we know who He is.

The Crown and The Cross

John 19:1-3,8-11,14-16, "Then Pilate took Jesus and had him flogged. The soldiers twisted together a crown of thorns and put it on his head. They clothed him in a purple robe and went up to him again and again, saying, "Hail, king of the Jews!" And they slapped him in the face... When Pilate heard this, he was even more afraid, and he went back inside the palace. "Where do you come from?" he asked Jesus, but Jesus gave him no answer.

"Do you refuse to speak to me?" Pilate said. "Don't you realize I have power either to free you or to crucify you?" Jesus answered, "You would have no power over me if it were not given to you from above. Therefore the one who handed me over to you is guilty of a greater sin..." It was the day of

Preparation of the Passover; it was about noon. "Here is your king," Pilate said to the Jews. But they shouted, "Take him away! Take him away! Crucify him!" "Shall I crucify your king?" Pilate asked. "We have no king but Caesar," the chief priests answered. Finally Pilate handed him over to them to be crucified. So the soldiers took charge of Jesus."'

Usually, when a king is crowned, it is with a crown of gold and jewels.

This King was crowned with thorns.

Usually, when a king is crowned, they sit on their throne.

But this King of Kings, Jesus Christ, when He is crowned, hangs on His cross.

Our King makes the cross a throne.

Jesus makes the altar a throne.

There are several themes to look at the grand narrative of the Bible story. Some summarize the Bible through the major lens or theme of relationships, a kingdom, covenants, redemption, etc. There are several motifs that work to summarize the major themes of Scripture and they inter-relate to one another.

It was difficult for me to reconcile through years of Bible study how the themes of the kingdom of God and of redemption came together. But it was when I saw it all through the cross that the beauty of this mystery came together.

Our God has chosen to be known by the place of sacrifice. God has eternally linked Himself to this place of execution and suffering.

The kingdom is about power, glory, and the return of Christ. The kingdom reign of Christ is in our hearts now, which we will fully experience upon His return and establishment of His kingdom's fullness on the earth.

The cross is about suffering, offering and the altar. In the cross, we see that the self-sacrificial love of Christ is what God's kingdom is all about.

After Jesus receives His beatings and the nasty crown of thorns puncturing His head, He stands trial with Pilate. Pilate represents the power of King Caesar locally in Israel. He has the power to save Jesus or have Him killed.

But this exchange is chilling.

Jesus is undaunted. As He faces His death, He has the upper hand.

Pilate and the crowd have allegiance to the throne of Caesar, but Jesus knows that His being laid on the altar is about to fulfill the eternal plan of heaven's throne.

The Apostles and Early Followers of Christ

Acts 7:59-60, "While they were stoning him, Stephen prayed, "Lord Jesus, receive my spirit." Then he fell on his knees and cried out, "Lord, do not hold this sin against them." When he said this, he fell asleep."

The very life and pattern of the apostles was a call to lay down their lives in suffering in the pattern of their Lord. Jesus told the disciples that they would experience the same type of sufferings He did.

As Jesus' life went the way of the altar, so did all the apostles. They suffered greatly and were tortured or executed for their allegiance to Jesus (only John wasn't executed, but He was tortured and exiled).

Stephen was one of the seven chosen to serve in Acts 6. He was not an apostle, but a deacon, and the first martyr for Christ.

After teaching a crowd, they got angry and charged to stone him. At his death, he prays basically two of the exact prayers to Jesus that Jesus prayed to the Father on the cross; "Receive my spirit" and "Do not hold this sin against them."

As Jesus advanced the purpose of God on the altar, so the early followers of Jesus did the same.

Paul even went as far as saying to the Colossians, "Now I rejoice in what I am suffering for you, and I fill up in my flesh what is still lacking in regard to Christ's afflictions, for the sake of his body, which is the church."

The altar was not just a place for Jesus; it is actually the way we continue to fulfill the purpose of His suffering as His body in the earth.

> **The altar was not just a place for Jesus; it is actually the way we continue to fulfill the purpose of His suffering as His body in the earth.**

Shattering the Power of Hell

1 Corinthians 2:8, "None of the rulers of this age understood it, for if they had, they would not have crucified the Lord of glory."

Colossians 2:13-15, "When you were dead in your sins and in the uncircumcision of your flesh, God made you alive with Christ. He forgave us all our sins, having canceled the charge of our legal indebtedness, which stood against us and condemned us; he has taken it away, nailing it to the cross. And having disarmed the powers and authorities, he made a public spectacle of them, triumphing over them by the cross."

The altar of the cross not only altered humanity, it shook the powers of hell. Paul wrote to the Corinthians that if the rulers of the world knew what would be accomplished through the cross, they would not have crucified Jesus.

The word for rulers not only refers to earthly political powers, but also to demonic or dark spiritual powers. Paul continues this revelation in Colossians that the cross was the place that disarmed demonic powers and authorities.

The cross was an altar of sacrifice that paid for our sins, but also destroyed the works of Satan and his minions.

The Church

Hebrews 13:10-16 "We have an altar from which those who minister at the tabernacle have no right to eat. The high priest carries the blood of animals into the Most Holy Place as a sin offering, but the bodies are burned outside the camp. And so Jesus also suffered outside the city gate to make the people holy through his own blood. Let us, then, go to him outside the camp, bearing the disgrace he bore. For here we do not have an enduring city, but we are looking for the city that is to come. Through Jesus, therefore, let us continually offer to God a sacrifice of praise---the fruit of lips that openly profess his name. And do not forget to do good and to share with others, for with such sacrifices God is pleased."

The word altar is not used many times in the New Testament.

The book of Hebrews shows how Jesus is better than the types of the Old Covenant. Jesus is better than the patriarchs of faith, angels, offerings, sacrifices, priests, and the tabernacle because they all find their fulfillment in Him. Jesus was the offering that paid for our sins once and for all.

```
Usually, when a king is crowned, it is with
        a crown of gold and jewels.
      This King was crowned with thorns.
Usually, when a king is crowned, they sit on
                their throne.
 But this King of Kings, Jesus Christ, when
      He is crowned, hangs on His cross.
       Our King makes the cross a throne.
```

His sacrifice on the altar was the end of sacrifice. The altar in the Old Covenant was fulfilled on the cross.

The writer of Hebrews says we have an altar as believers that is superior to the altar of the Old Covenant. In the Old Covenant, on the Day of Atonement, the priests burnt the sin offering completely and did not enjoy it. But in the New Covenant, by faith, we have a spiritual altar though the cross where we can continually feast on the sacrifice that Jesus made for us.

Where the book of Hebrews teaches us the end of ritual sacrifice, we learn about the sacrifice at the end of sacrifice: the sacrifice of praise.

What do we do as the church because of Christ laying on the altar for us? We praise Him and thank Him with our words. Our worship and adoration of Him in song and in prayers is the sacrifice that pleases God. Additionally, out of that place of praising God, we please Him when we do good to others and share with them.

1 Corinthians 10:15-21, "I speak to sensible people; judge for yourselves what I say. Is not the cup of thanksgiving for which we give thanks a participation in the blood of Christ? And is not the bread that we break a participation in the body of Christ? Because there is one loaf, we, who are many, are one body, for we all share the one loaf. Consider the people of Israel: Do not those who eat the sacrifices participate in the altar? Do I mean then that food sacrificed to an idol is anything, or that an idol is anything? No, but the sacrifices of pagans are offered to demons, not to God, and I do not want you to be participants with demons. You cannot drink the cup of the Lord and the cup of demons too; you cannot have a part in both the Lord's table and the table of demons."

During the time of the writing of the New Testament, public altars to idols were common in the culture. Paul warns the Corinthians that going to eat a meal at the altar of an idol is to participate with demons. Christians need to be careful of idolatry because even as a Christian, these altars can open you to demonic oppression. There is demonic power at altars of idols.

Paul is concerned about them opening themselves to evil spirits and grieving the Lord. But we also learn that not only do we participate with demons at altars of idols, but we can participate in the blood and body of Christ through the altar of the Lord in holy communion.

Now at the time Paul wrote this, there is not a record of a literal altar being used. Even later, in 1 Corinthians 11, we see that communion is during a love feast, which was a meal for the church to gather around a table. But the real connections between the presence of Christ or the presence of demons is based upon the altars where we fellowship.

The Altar in Heaven

Revelation 6:9, "When he opened the fifth seal, I saw under the altar the souls of those who had been slain because of the word of God and the testimony they had maintained."

Revelation 8:5, "Then the angel took the censer, filled it with fire from the altar, and hurled it on the earth; and there came peals of thunder, rumblings, flashes of lightning and an earthquake."

The altar in heaven is the place of divine activity in the book of Revelation. There is a connection between the altar and both the suffering and prayers of the saints.

As Jesus advanced the purpose of God on the altar, so the early followers of Jesus did the same.

In heaven, the altar is a place where martyrs for Christ dwell. Their lives as an offering unto God because of Christ, give them an important place in heaven to cry out for God's vengeance on the earth. Every soul that dies for their faith and love for Christ has a beautiful place and reward in heaven. When they die in suffering as their Lord, their lives become tied to the heavenly altar to carry out God's purposes by participation in heaven.

Not only do those in heaven who are martyrs participate in the altar, but the church on earth participates in heaven's altar through earthly altars of prayer. Altars still shape history, and they will until the very end.

Just like the Old Covenant altars that connected earth with heaven, when we give ourselves to prayer, our prayers are rising before the throne of heaven where angels mix them with incense and fire from the altar. These prayers before the throne offered with fire from the altar are hurled back to the earth as answered prayer.

Earthly thrones don't have this kind of power to move the throne of heaven, but altars do.

Altars still shape history, and they will until the very end.

The Altar and the Throne

Revelation 5:6, "Then I saw a Lamb, looking as if it had been slain, standing at the center of the throne, encircled by the four living creatures and the elders. The Lamb had seven horns and seven eyes, which are the seven spirits of God sent out into all the earth."

Where on the cross, Jesus made the altar a throne, in heaven Jesus made the throne an altar. This is the significance and beauty of Jesus being the Lamb slain before the foundation of the world. It was always God's plan to reconcile all things through the cross of Jesus. All that Jesus did was to bring humanity into peace with God through the shedding of His blood so we could have eternal life and fellowship with God forever.

Philippians said of Jesus, "Who, being in very nature God, did not consider equality with God something to be used to his own advantage; rather, he made himself nothing by taking the very nature of a servant, being made in human likeness. And being found in appearance as a man, he humbled himself by becoming obedient to death— even death on a cross! Therefore God exalted him to the highest place and gave him the name that is above every name, that at the name of Jesus every knee should bow, in heaven and on earth and under the earth, and every tongue acknowledge that Jesus Christ is Lord, to the glory of God the Father[1]*."*

> **Where on the cross, Jesus made the altar a throne, in heaven Jesus made the throne an altar.**

Jesus' humiliation led to His exaltation. The crucifixion means nothing without the resurrection. If Jesus did not rise from the dead, He would not be exalted and we would be stuck in our sins.

But our God is the suffering Savior. He is seated on heaven's throne and His name is exalted above every name because He was the sin offering on the altar for us. But even in His victory and exaltation after His crucifixion and resurrection, He still bears the marks of His suffering as the Lamb of God.

Altars are over thrones because Jesus is over the throne, the Lamb Slain on the altar.

In heaven forever, Jesus will bear the marks of His suffering.

In heaven forever, the altar is over the throne.

In heaven forever, Jesus has made the altar and throne one.

Through His sacrifice, He is glorified now and forever.

Summary

The New Covenant altar is about what Christ has fulfilled. As I've heard before, "The Old Covenant is the New Covenant concealed, and the New Covenant is the Old Covenant revealed."

This is true of the narrative of altars throughout the Scriptures. The

---

1. Philippians 2:6-11

New Covenant reveals and fulfills what happens through the cross of Jesus as an offering on the altar for us. The blessings of the altar are now applied in our lives by faith in what Jesus has done on the cross. Here is a summary of what we learn through New Testament altars. Altars are:

- fulfilled through Jesus being the Lamb of God slain for us.
- fulfilled in the person of Jesus Christ and His cross where He was made an offering for our sin.
- a place of repentance, humility and prayers.
- also in heaven.
- a place to connect earth and heaven.
- exalted over thrones.

Chapter 4

Restoring the Altar of the Heart

I was recently in an on-line group call with Pastor Jon Tyson who leads Church of the City, New York. There is a prayer movement being birthed in his church, where he runs a conference called *Altars*, which empowers and equips churches to pursue a culture and lifestyle of prayer.

He told us a story about a time years ago, when he took his family on a trip, a revival tour of 17 cities around the world. When he visited the Hebrides islands in Scotland, he got to read the diary of the evangelist Duncan Campbell, who was chosen by God to lead an incredible revival in the mid-1900s. He came across the four altars that Campbell said must be built or rebuilt to birth revival or spiritual awakening.

1. The Altar of the Heart
2. The Altar of the Home
3. The Altar of the Church
4. The Altar of the Region

First Love Fire

Restoring the altar of the heart is all about the first love you have for Jesus and letting it burn brightly and deeply.

I grew up in a pastor's home. My hippie dad was radically saved from a life of drug and alcohol addiction. He met my mom at a tavern in Seattle when the rock band Heart was playing. She was a partially committed Catholic.

After the meeting and in the middle of a breakdown, my dad was at a family member's house, and he read David Wilkerson's *The Cross and the Switchblade* in one sitting. He gave his life to Jesus as a result.

Sometime shortly thereafter, one of the gang members in the book he read, Israel Narvaez, was in the Seattle area at the church my dad was attending, Westgate Chapel. My Mom heard him preach, and she was born again.

My parents got married and my dad ended up going to Seattle Bible College. His church hired him to be a staff evangelist because he told everyone he met about Jesus. After making a big impact in his home church through evangelism and signs and wonders, my dad planted our church Sonrise Christian Center (Sonrise Chapel at the time), when I was six years old.

I grew up in a good home with parents who loved Jesus. They modeled a life of devotion and living at the altar, whether at home or at church; they were disciplined in their prayer lives. We read the Bible as a family and prayed regularly.

They were authentic and faithful Christians who were vulnerable about their weaknesses and set an amazing example of always believing God.

I struggled as a pastor's kid who went to Christian school to fully live out my faith. Outwardly, I achieved good grades and seemed like the average all-American church kid, I suppose. I was so afraid of what people thought about me at a young age and wanted to impress people with my successes and achievements. I lived in secret moral compromise from age twelve to twenty, despite having some amazing God encounters in my early teens.

When I was 12, in 1993, during the Super Bowl half-time show, my parents turned off the television because my dad had been talking to us about the baptism in the Holy Spirit. While Michael Jackson was entertaining the nation, I was in my parents' bedroom with my family, weeping and speaking in tongues as my parents prayed for me.

The next year, at 13, I had this strong desire to preach a message to my Christian school about the love of God from 1 John 4.

I preached at the middle and high school chapel. I was so overcome with emotion and the heart of God that I crumpled up my notes and preached for maybe twenty minutes straight from my heart. I did altar calls and had an overwhelming response with both my peers and the older students in high school.

But it was in this same season, that I started to live a double life of hypocrisy and ended up caring more about what other people thought about me than pleasing God.

I had moments at camps and special church conferences where I had deep spiritual and emotional encounters with God. My dad used to speak at a youth camp at Lake Entiat, and my youth group went to Camp Berachah. The power of the Holy Spirit was present in such tangible ways at virtually every camp I went to. I saw God answer prayers, save the lost and work miracles. The presence of God marked my life in such ways that even though I struggled through these years, I longed to come back and experience Him in those ways.

When I was twenty years old, I had a life-changing encounter with Jesus in deliverance; I felt like I really understood for the first time what it meant to be saved and have a personal relationship with Him. With compromise out of my life, I began to confess my former sins, go to prayer meetings, tell people about Jesus and get into my church, or any church for that matter, as much as I could.

It felt so amazing to be free. Even though I had to renew my mind and repair my broken identity, I felt so alive and had such an abiding love for Jesus.

In Revelation 2, we see that Jesus was measuring the temperature of His church's love for Him in Ephesus. It's important to remember how we came to faith and what our first love for Jesus is all about.

The altar of the heart starts with cultivating a first love for Him. It can't just be an emotional type of love, but a sacrificial love. It's not just a feeling of love, but a love that orders and prizes Jesus as first and most. He wants no rival in our lives and it's often in our first stages of salvation that the first love fire on the altar of our hearts is stoked the hottest.

The Gospel

As I grew and matured in my love for Jesus in my twenties, I was confronting major lies I had believed about performance.

During the time I attended Bible college, I had a pretty heated discussion with my dad because I was so full of shame from my past; I was ready to quit ministry before I even started. I was seriously weighing the option of just dropping out of Bible college. In this specific discussion, I was convinced I had failed too much in my past and would fail people even more in the future.

My dad asked me a question that changed the trajectory of my heart.

He asked, "Son, do you believe what Jesus did on the cross is enough to forgive you and free you from all your sin, or do you still think there is something else you have to do?"

In my heightened state of emotions, I blurted, "There's got to be something else."

As soon as it came out of my mouth, I almost gasped. I was shocked by my own answer. In all the pressure I was under spiritually, mentally, and emotionally, the lie that I could somehow add to the blood of Jesus for my own righteousness was squeezed right out of me.

It wasn't an overnight change, but I started seeing my life through the lens of the gospel from that point forward.

The only way to cultivate an abiding first love for Jesus on the altar of our heart is to be convinced that God loves us first.

We only love God because He first loves us.

The Christian life begins with the revelation of Jesus and the power of what He has done for us.

In Romans, the Bible says, ""But God demonstrates his own love for us in this: While we were still sinners, Christ died for us."[1]

The gospel, or good news, for all of us is that Christ did not die for

---

1. Romans 5:8

us when we were righteous and could offer Him anything He had need of. He demonstrated His love for us while we were sinners. He died for us at our lowest moment, not our best.

When this Biblical revelation from God illuminates your heart, you will never be the same again.

The fire on the altar of our hearts will only burn when it is sustained in gospel love. The love in our heart for God is not something we create; it's something we respond to.

Our love to God is a response to the self-sacrificial love of Jesus. The gospel is not just a proclamation, so those lost might believe, but it's a message for the believer to feast on daily.

The love of God through the gospel is the enduring fuel for the altar of our heart. Our God spread Himself on the altar. This changes everything and our love is a response.

The love in our heart for God is not something we create; it's something we respond to.

The Cross Shaped Life

In one sense, we cannot think too greatly of the depths of God's love for us, but in another, if we only focus on the gospel about our identity in justification, we miss out on the invitation to become Christlike in sanctification.

God has a vision for your life and it's not only that you are forgiven and go to heaven when you die, but that you become like Jesus. The apostle Paul's aim was not only to convert as many people to Christ as He could but was to "present everyone fully mature in Christ."[2]

In my own walk with Jesus, I learned Jesus wanted to deepen my

---

2. Colossians 1:28

love through learning obedience in suffering. After all, the Scripture says of Jesus, "Son though he was, he learned obedience from what he suffered."[3]

God has a vision for your life and it's not only that you are forgiven and go to heaven when you die, but that you become like Jesus.

When I really felt like I got a hold of my identity in Christ and knew the depths of God's love for me, life was so much fuller and even easier. I woke up every day in my twenties and thirties, knowing I was loved through the gospel.

I was helping people, loving my family and enjoying a growing ministry of preaching the gospel and seeing people set free. But when I hit my late thirties, I was about to be tried like I have never before experienced.

In 2019, my wife and I were almost done with a multi-year transition plan to lead the church my parents planted in 1986. A few months before we transitioned into leadership, my mild gut health issues I'd struggled with over the years flared up to become a major health crisis.

I went from almost 180 pounds to 133 pounds in a short period of time. I looked skeletal, and I was totally depleted of energy.

I had seen many healing miracles, so I got a lot of prayer. I saw various doctors and specialists, but my results were always inconclusive.

I had no reserves physically, and I was getting barely any sleep. Some of my friends that died at a young age from chronic disease had some of the same symptoms as I did. I felt like I was going crazy from anxious thoughts and was afraid I would die young.

---

3. Hebrews 5:8

Somehow, I trucked ahead, with the love of my wife, family, friends, and a wise nutritionist, Dr. Bisci. I slowly healed that year.

I was pretty good after year one of a healthier lifestyle and started to put weight back on after 18 months.

But in early 2020, Covid hit.

Our church attendance was cut in half. Many of our church people left the state. We lost half our staff and half our elders due to life transitions, new job opportunities for people in other states and budget cuts.

Everything I said in this time was too political, or not political enough. I didn't want to open my emails or go to church on Sunday for the constant stream of unsolicited advice and criticism.

Our marriage had been relatively easy for the first 15 years and after becoming lead pastors, we both started experiencing incredible tension, emotional challenges, and spiritual warfare.

Thankfully, the pressure pushed us deeper into prayer with one another and we received strength from great spiritual fathers and mothers, and wise counsel. We are deeper in love now after 20 years through the refining fire of trials.

Stressful leadership challenges mounted up during the first five years of being lead pastors as well. My dad told me he didn't have to deal with these types of crises very often, and I was having multiple crises and leadership challenges occur in the same week sometimes.

Through the stress of it all, I wanted to just give up.

I was depressed and overwhelmed a lot of the time. I wasn't suicidal, but one counselor told me I was having escapist fantasies where my mind would randomly drift into getting injured or killed in various types of accidents.

The pain of quitting felt so much better than continuing.

One day I told Grace to call my dad so he could come over and help me write a letter of resignation.

Well, I was talking with them and pouring out my heart, and we prayed. I saw a picture in my mind of Jesus reaching out His hand to me and beckoning me to follow Him. My heart knew in that moment that if I gave up on ministry at this point, I wouldn't be following Jesus; but if I continued to follow Him in the call on my life, I would be with Him.

At that moment, I surrendered and said, "Lord, if I get more of You for staying, then I won't quit."

Jesus said this is what it looks like to follow Him, "Whoever wants to be my disciple must deny themselves and take up their cross and follow me. For whoever wants to save their life will lose it, but whoever loses their life for me and for the gospel will save it. What good is it for someone to gain the whole world, yet forfeit their soul? Or what can anyone give in exchange for their soul? If anyone is ashamed of me and my words in this adulterous and sinful generation, the Son of Man will be ashamed of them when he comes in his Father's glory with the holy angels.""[4]

I learned through this season of hardships and heartache to not try and avoid suffering.

I fell in love with the cross. I don't believe that God makes us depressed or anxious, but we will walk through various types of hardships in life.

I found that Christ met me with an unusual grace in my suffering at the place of His suffering. In the cross, I realized that Jesus really knew me in my pain, but I also realized that I knew something about His pain in my suffering.

The fellowship with Him has become so rich and powerful. The greater the crushing, the richer the oil and the sweeter the wine flows.

The greater the crushing, the richer the oil and the sweeter the wine flows.

Most of my life I was knowing God through the power of His resurrection, but I came to know Him so much deeper through the fellowship of His sufferings.[5]

---

4. Mark 8:34-38
5. Philippians 3:10

You might want to represent the Christian life with a heart, a hand, a smiley face, or a peace sign. But the Christian life is cross shaped.

We don't get to pick the shape of our Christianity. Following Jesus is not only about love, holiness, morals, service, etc. Following Jesus is about taking up your cross. Christianity, being a "little-Christ," is the way of the altar. The cross was Christ's altar, and we are called in the way of our Master to be on the altar.

After the greatest treatise on the salvation that Christ freely bestows on us by His amazing grace, the Apostle Paul tells us this is how we respond, "Therefore, I urge you, brothers and sisters, in view of God's mercy, to offer your bodies as a living sacrifice, holy and pleasing to God—this is your true and proper worship. Do not conform to the pattern of this world, but be transformed by the renewing of your mind. Then you will be able to test and approve what God's will is—his good, pleasing and perfect will."[6]

After 11 chapters of Biblical revelation on what it means to be forgiven and justified by faith, sanctified, the object of God's love by which nothing can separate us and many other spiritual blessings, Paul says we have one response: be a living sacrifice. He calls this our "true and proper worship" and in the New King James Version our "reasonable service."

> **But the Christian life is cross shaped. We don't get to pick the shape of our Christianity.**

Our only reasonable and true response for the one who gave us His all, is to respond in kind. We offer Him our life. Being a living sacrifice is where we perpetually offer our lives to the Lord in a state of surrender.

This posture of embracing the cross and laying our lives on the altar

---

6. Romans 12:1-2

brings glory to God in worship and causes us to be transformed through mind renewal. This kind of self emptying and embracing the path of the cross causes us to truly live out the will of God for our lives. Which is not so much about our destiny of what we do, but the destination of becoming more like Jesus.

We aren't to have a morbid view of self-inflicted suffering or punishment. We need a healthy view that suffering will happen as followers of Jesus and instead of resisting it we lay our lives down like He did, surrendering all for His glory. The cross shaped life is about conformity to Christlikeness where we are separate from the world in holiness.

We die to self by repenting of sin, not tolerating compromise in our lives and adopting godliness in the place of worldliness.

Christianity, being a "little-Christ," is the way of the altar. The cross was Christ's altar, and we are called in the way of our Master to be on the altar.

Pray Continually

The path of self-denial, carrying the cross and surrendering on the altar in the Christian life starts with a heart posture but is only sustained by a life of prayer.

The call to the altar for the Christian is a call to a faithful life of prayer. If Jesus had a secret to how He carried out His ministry, it was His prayer life.

If we look at heroes of the faith who shaped history for Christ, it was their prayer life.

Jesus responded to the invitation of His heavenly Father morning by morning. Isaiah prophesies in one of the Servant Songs about Jesus the Messiah and how He would carry out His mission in the world.

""The Lord God has given Me The tongue of the learned, That I should know how to speak A word in season to him who is weary. He awakens Me morning by morning, He awakens My ear To hear as the learned. The Lord God has opened My ear; And I was not rebellious, Nor did I turn away. I gave My back to those who struck Me, And My cheeks to those who plucked out the beard; I did not hide My face from shame and spitting. "For the Lord God will help Me; Therefore I will not be disgraced; Therefore I have set My face like a flint, And I know that I will not be ashamed. He is near who justifies Me; Who will contend with Me? Let us stand together. Who is My adversary? Let him come near Me. Surely the Lord God will help Me; Who is he who will condemn Me?..."[7]

How potent. Jesus had the tongue of the learned because He had an awakened ear. Jesus responded to the call from His Father to draw away and be alone with Him. We see this pattern throughout the gospels of Jesus' life and ministry. He is constantly drawing away to solitude to practice the presence of God.

In Isaiah's prophecy we see that this is where Jesus died to His self will and was willing to lay down His life on the altar for humanity. Isaiah says that He gave His back to those who struck Him, His cheeks to those who plucked His beard and His face to those who spit on and shamed Him.

This is the language of surrender.

Jesus died at the word of the Lord in prayer before He ever got to the cross.

Then He goes on to say He will not be disgraced or ashamed. He says He will not be contended with, have an adversary or be condemned. This is all a prophecy about surrender leading to the cross for Jesus.

Jesus died at the word of the Lord in prayer before He ever got to the cross. If the cross is anything, it's a place of disgrace, shame,

---

7. Isaiah 50:4-9 NKJV

contention, adversaries and condemnation, yet Jesus says none of these things will touch Him in suffering. He had already yielded to the altar in prayer before He went to the cross.

The real battle for Jesus' obedience wasn't the cross, it was in the garden of Gethsemane. Jesus took Peter, James, and John to pray with Him after the last supper and before His arrest. He wanted prayer with His closest friends in His hour of suffering more than anything else. He knew His time was drawing near to die. He was in such anguish. He sweat drops of blood in the garden. He was grieved that in His hour of need, His disciples could not pray with Him for one hour.

And it was in this place that His human will submitted to His Divine will, ""Going a little farther, he fell with his face to the ground and prayed, "My Father, if it is possible, may this cup be taken from me. Yet not as I will, but as you will.""[8]

This is the surrender that Isaiah prophesied about the One who had the awakened ear. Prayer allows us to yield to the altar, as we see in the example of Jesus.

Prayer is the currency of heaven.

This invitation of Jesus in His hour of need to His closest friends also shows us that Jesus longs for comfort from His followers to minister to the ache in His heart.

Mother Basilea, in her book *My All For Him*, so beautifully teaches us about a way to sustain the fire of prayer in the altar of our hearts is to come to prayer not for our own needs but to minister to the needs in God's heart.

If Jesus is the same yesterday, today and forever, then His heart still aches for the injustice and evil in the world and ultimately for those who are separated from Him. Prayer that matures in love becomes a place

---

8. Matthew 26:39

where we go to ask the Lord if He wants to come and find comfort as we help carry His burden.

Jesus' whole life was characterized this way. He didn't just end His ministry in prayer at the cross because times got tough. His ministry was birthed in a time of prayer and testing in the wilderness.

Jesus shows us that prayer and fasting in the midst of trials and testing releases a type of impartation in our lives. Jesus went into His wilderness test led by the Holy Spirit and after 40 days of prayer and fasting, as well as facing the devil, He left the wilderness empowered by the Spirit.

Prayer and fasting unlocks our spiritual potential. It creates a resolve in us to die to self, be empty of self and fills us with God's Spirit.

When the disciples couldn't cast out a demon of a tormented boy, Jesus showed them they could get breakthroughs in these tough cases by prayer and fasting. Paul the apostle tells us to "pray without ceasing."[9]

Jude tells us "But you, dear friends, by building yourselves up in your most holy faith and praying in the Holy Spirit."[10]

A continual life of prayer will rebuild and renew the fire on the altar of our heart. Prayer is the activation of our faith, and along with obedience, is how we apply God's Word to our heart. Prayer is the currency of heaven.

As Oswald Chambers said, "Prayer does not fit us for the greater work, prayer is the greater work."[11]

> **Prayer that matures in love becomes a place where we go to ask the Lord if He wants to come and find comfort as we help carry His burden.**

---

9. 1 Thessalonians 5:17 NKJV
10. Jude 1:20
11. https://utmost.org/classic/greater-works-classic/

Impartation

Not only does our own prayer life build a fire on the altar of prayer in our lives, so do others' prayers for us. Paul wrote to his true son in the faith Timothy, "For this reason I remind you to fan into flame the gift of God, which is in you through the laying on of my hands. For the Spirit God gave us does not make us timid, but gives us power, love and self-discipline."[12]

Paul describes here that there is a resident fire inside of Timothy that He could fan into flame or stir up. This resident flame within was a gift of God which was ignited through the laying on of hands.

When Grace and I were desperate for God to move in our church and in our own lives after a few tough years of trials as lead pastors, we attended a nearby conference. A young man named Raul Dimov, who had been saved through our evangelistic ministry that we hosted in our region seven years before, was hosting a conference in the same building he got saved in.

We wanted to go and support him, but I was also hungry to receive from God. We were worn out, but I really felt like being there just to celebrate what God was doing was important. But as the event drew closer, I was in all out desperation and brokenness for a touch from God.

It was inconvenient to go that weekend, but I'm so thankful we did.

On Friday night, Randy Clark brought a message on the power of impartation. I'd heard him share that teaching at least a couple of times prior, and he had even laid hands on me in prayer before as well.

But as he finished up his message, the power of God hit my body right there in my seat. I usually cry a little in the presence of God, but this time I started having jolts of God's power go through my body. I ran to the altar and dropped to the floor as my hands shook uncontrollably and I was balled up on the floor, weeping, with the power of God moving over my body. I was repenting, yielding, and surrendering. In that encounter, God gave me instructions for our church and ministry that we have walked out for the past two years with incredible fruit.

---

12. 2 Timothy 1:6-7

I had never experienced a touch from God like this in my life.

I got home that night and my wife said, "I thought you said if we went to this meeting, we were going to receive a touch from God. But only you did."

I told her we should go back on Saturday night even though our schedule was so full. She decided to go one more night and the power of God came upon Grace sovereignly without anyone laying hands on her. I don't know if I have ever seen someone receive a touch of God like that before. For at least an hour or two, as Heidi Baker prayed, my wife shook on the floor and wept before the Lord.

We tried to leave even after being released twice and as I got her off the floor to walk her down the aisle, it was like an invisible hand came and pushed her to the floor where she continued to encounter the glory of God.

We finally got to bed close to midnight, and after I had fallen asleep, I awoke to our bed shaking as Grace continued to encounter the manifest presence of God. These encounters we read about in the lives of Jonathan and Sarah Edwards, the Cane Ridge revival, John Wesley's meetings and other revivals in church history were happening to us.

We woke up the next day with the power of God physically resting upon us and went to church. The entire service was overcome with the presence of God and experienced the same impartation we received.

These types of encounters are continuing.

They are leading to a conviction of sin, a spirit of repentance and prayer, the saving of the lost, healing, deliverance, and a flow of prophetic gifts.

There is a fire in the life of a believer through the laying on of hands.

We have lost the significance of the doctrine of the laying on of hands. The author of Hebrews puts the laying on of hands as an elementary doctrine and as significant as the doctrines of repentance, faith, baptisms, the resurrection of the dead and eternal judgment.[13]

Many Christians live without the power of the Holy Spirit living in them, while this flame of fire, this baptism of love and power, is available.

---

13. Hebrews 6:1-2 NKJV

If only we pray for one another more, and lay hands on one another, we might impart the power and gift of God to one another through fervent prayer.

If only we long for the touch of God and seek to receive from those who have a fire burning in them of the Holy Spirit. May God ignite in us a fire on the altar of our hearts through the power of His love, His gospel, His cross and a life of prayer and impartation.

Chapter 5

Restoring the Family Altar

Some of the strongest memories of my childhood have to do with the altars in my home. Almost every morning when I woke up to get ready for school, I would see my mom kneeling at our couch in the living room with her hands folded in prayer and her Bible laid open in front of her.

We regularly had Bible reading and prayer times at night as a family that we called devotions.

When I visited my dad during the week at church as a young man, he was often laying at the altar in the front of our sanctuary with his Bible open in front of him as he cried out to God.

I thank God I was raised at the altar.

Families of the Covenant

All throughout the Old Testament Scriptures as we looked at earlier, we see that families of the covenant encountered God at altars. Abraham, Isaac and Jacob all worshiped and honored God at altars throughout key moments in their life stories. God is a covenant keeping God and the first covenants He gave in the earth were in a family context of Adam and Eve, Noah and the patriarchs of Israel.

When the Bible narrative gets to Moses, something very intense takes place. After God had called Moses at the burning bush to be the deliverer for His Israel, the Bible says, "At a lodging place on the way, the Lord met Moses and was about to kill Him."[1]

Why would God almost kill the one He chose to lead His people out of slavery and into the promised land?

We get a sense of why, when His wife Zipporah, who is a Middianite, reacts quickly by taking out a knife and circumcises her son. She tosses her son's foreskin on the ground at the feet of Moses. God suddenly pulls back His judgement and spares Moses at this action. God is saying that Moses cannot lead His people if He isn't leading his family. He cannot change the world if he cannot change his own home.

God wasn't going to let Moses lead His covenant people if the sign of the covenant wasn't honored in his own family.

I often feel that Christians believe the world changes through massive events that tackle the big issues of our culture, but I believe that massive change comes through the simple restoration of family altars. The last verse of the Old Testament tells us that unless the hearts of fathers are turned to their children and the hearts of children to their fathers, then the Lord strikes the earth with a curse.[2]

Wherever there is an epidemic of brokenness and pain in our culture as seen in addiction, abuse, crime and poverty, there are often not only personal sins but broken homes. Repairing the altar of our families is where the power to heal and change culture lies.

The Family Altar

One of the most powerful things we can do as a Christian family is have time together in the presence of the Lord regularly.

At different seasons of life, we have enjoyed different rhythms of spending time with our children in Scripture reading and prayer. Earlier in our lives, we read the Bible together almost every night and prayed with our children before bedtime. Grace was brilliant and came up with

---

1. Exodus 4:24
2. Malachi 4:6

creative ways to do songs and memorize Scriptures. As our kids have grown, they follow the same daily Bible reading plan as us, and on our weekly Sabbath, we have a special time at our family altar.

We aren't perfect about a weekly Sabbath, but we try to be consistent. It's something our family really enjoys, and we typically end it with an evening at the altar.

Our time starts with singing some worship songs. Then we read and discuss Scripture, unpacking it and sharing our favorite insights. After Bible reading, we do thankfulness prayer, which involves us going around in a circle and sharing three things we are thankful for as a prayer to God. "Thank You God for …" When thankfulness prayer is over I pray the Aaronic blessing over my family, "The Lord bless you and keep you; the Lord make his face shine on you and be gracious to you; the Lord turn his face toward you and give you peace."[3] This is followed by a blessing I learned from Jewish tradition to pray over my daughters, "I pray the Lord bless you Justus like Ephraim and Manasseh and the Lord bless you Hailey, Emma and Addi like Sarah, Rebekah, Rachel and Leah."[4]

This rhythm of daily Bible reading and weekly altar time creates a rhythm of spiritual devotion and is something we all look forward to. Sometimes we deal with bad attitudes, or even as a dad, I can feel extra vulnerable and irritable when I set out to do devotions as a family and something goes wrong.

Even when things don't go perfectly, there is such a powerful fruit to it. Grace and I received these traditions at the altar from our parents, and now we are passing them down to the next generation.

Our children know that our home and our family are devoted to Christ above all else.

Discipleship

The family altar should be some place in your home where you regularly

---

3. Numbers 6:24-26
4. https://reformjudaism.org/beliefs-practices/prayers-blessings/shabbat-and-holiday-blessings-blessing-over-children

meet with God together in prayer. But more than just saying prayers, the family altar becomes a central part of how you disciple the next generation.

Children of the covenant in Israel were to be instructed by their parents. There was a declaration of faith in Israel that became an ancient way of discipleship for the Israelites in their own home. It was called the Shema in Israel, which means to hear. "Hear, O Israel: The Lord our God, the Lord is one. Love the Lord your God with all your heart and with all your soul and with all your strength. These commandments that I give you today are to be on your hearts. Impress them on your children. Talk about them when you sit at home and when you walk along the road, when you lie down and when you get up. Tie them as symbols on your hands and bind them on your foreheads. Write them on the doorframes of your houses and on your gates."[5]

Again, I believe the family altar ought to be a literal place in the home where you consistently meet with the Lord together, but it has to be more than just a Bible study. To truly rebuild the altars of our homes we need to catechize our children.

The process of catechism seems to be stronger in mainline and historic Christian denominations. But what we see in Deuteronomy is that we must teach our children to hear the Word of the Lord all throughout their lives. We need to intentionally teach, confess, and meditate on the Scriptures with our children.

Our children's world should be shaped by the Word of God. On top of devotions, spend time reading books on theology and Scripture that help children have a basic understanding of Christianity.

Parents function as the main influence of their children's faith. Before there was a nation or a church, there was a family. The greatest strength to children's faith is not how great the kids or youth ministry in a church are, but how faithful their parents' faith is in shaping their own.

A key part of discipleship is not only teaching, but discipline. Discipline your children when they are unruly. Our children will not know our love for them if we don't create and enforce boundaries to protect

---

5. Deuteronomy 6:4-9

them and teach them the way to walk after the Lord. Character is formed at the altar in prayer and in the consequences our children face for sin, rebellion, and disobedience. All discipline should be out of love and not in harshness or anger. Even the Lord disciplines those He loves.[6] This is a powerful part of our discipleship.

Modeling

All of our teaching and instructing means little to nothing if we are not modeling the things we desire to see in our children. One thing I always appreciated about the pastors my dad brought on to work with him over the years is that they modeled the Christian life with joy and integrity. The pastors' families that I was raised around had the type of marriage and families that anyone would desire. No one has a perfect family, but we can have redeemed families built on Christ. That is what I witnessed, real Christians loving Jesus, loving their families, and loving their community.

These marriages and families that surrounded me as a young man were fun. They were spiritual, but not stuffy or fake. They loved prayer, the presence of God, and service. But they also knew how to have a good time and enjoy life.

This was true of my own home and Grace's as well.

One time I asked Graham Cooke how to help develop a culture of prayer, and he said to me, "Well, people typically do what they enjoy doing, right? So, figure out how to make prayer enjoyable."

I think that is the key to the family altar.

Make prayer, devotion, and following Jesus enjoyable. Bring your children into the adventure of prayer and obedience with you.

My friend Meesh Fomenko, an international evangelist, was raised in a large family from Moldova. His dad was an incredible minister of faith and all of his siblings serve the Lord.

Meesh's dad died at an early age but left a legacy for them by modeling faith and trust.

Meesh has told me story after story of God doing miracles in answer

---

6. Hebrews 12:6

to his father leading their family in prayer. One such story is that when they had no money, his father placed his wallet on a table and they marched around the table like it was the walls of Jericho, worshipping, praising, and thanking God. As a result, God provided miraculously and the whole family got to be in on the miracle of provision in God's response to answered prayer.

This is how I was raised.

I watched my parents model prayer, spiritual hunger, a loving marriage, forgiving people who hurt them, trusting God for provision, and seeing God work miracles in our lives.

When I was a youth pastor, I often had parents wanting more for their children spiritually. They wanted their children to do great things for God and take risks of faith. They would ask me how to get their kids more "on fire" for God.

Well, it's really simple. How are you modeling for your children a life of fire for God? If you want to see spiritual hunger in the next generation, then pursue God wholeheartedly in yours. Model a joyful and faithful pursuit of God and invite them into the abundant life you are living in Christ.

Modeling is not about doing everything with perfection, but with authenticity.

One of the most powerful things we can model is in our failures as parents. We show the humility of confessing our faults and asking for our children's forgiveness. The altar of the home cannot be built on religious exercises only, but also by maintaining healthy relationships with one another.

Another part of authenticity in what we model is when we share our testimonies about how Jesus helped us overcome various sins in our lives. Modeling authenticity and humility, as well as having a culture of blessing in your home, creates an environment where your children can confess their sins and temptations to you.

We don't make our children confess all their sins in front of their siblings or force them to do anything. We share openly about sensitive topics without shame and invite them into sharing with us privately when they have struggles. When they are not scolded or shamed for opening up, but rather, met with love, they learn about the power of grace and living without secrets.

Marriage and the Family Altar

Without honor in our relationships, our prayers will not be heard.

A family altar cannot be built on a fractured marriage. The Lord says for our prayers to be heard, we have to treat our marriages with honor.

"Husbands, in the same way be considerate as you live with your wives, and treat them with respect as the weaker partner and as heirs with you of the gracious gift of life, so that nothing will hinder your prayers."[7]

If I don't love my wife, not only does it set a bad example for my children, it robs me of answered prayer.

What a sobering truth, that my true spiritual vitality in prayer is inextricably linked to the grace I extend to my wife.

The key to a healthy family is marriage that is rich in God's love.

When a husband and wife are joined together, they become a one flesh union; in God, a husband and wife, the two become one. Jim and Eva Johnson, who are marriage ministry legends in our church, have helped couples restore and renew their marriages for over forty years. The thing I've learned the most from them is about this one flesh union in marriage. It is a spiritual union that is nourished spiritually in prayer.

When Grace and I were about to get married, many married couples who we looked up to and respected, even people with powerful ministries, told us the most difficult person for them to pray with was their spouse.

That grieved us and motivated us to learn to pray together. We resolved that starting on our honeymoon, and for the rest of our lives, we would pray together.

We pray for each other virtually every morning and every night. Through troubles and trials, we have learned to pray quickly when we

---

7. 1 Peter 3:7

don't know what to do. When our words to one another fail, our words to God on behalf of one another do not.

A strong family altar of prayer and devotion to Jesus is built on the strong prayer life of a husband and wife.

Blessing

I believe to have a strong altar in the home, we need a strong culture of blessing.

Earlier, I mentioned the power of praying the Aaronic blessing, also called the priestly blessing, on a weekly Sabbath rest day. A culture of blessing in our home must extend to everything we do.

"The tongue has the power of life and death, and those who love it will eat its fruit."[8]

Our children rise to the level of our blessing.

It's true of our marriage too.

How do you speak to your spouse and to your children?

How do you speak *about* them?

Speak life over them.

My wife is brilliant at blessing us even when there's tension, and she's great at shifting the atmosphere of a situation from discouraging to hopeful.

Our family will long to be around us regularly, and in the most important moments of life, when we speak blessing and life over them.

When we bless them, we are telling them who they are and who they are becoming in the world.

We must discipline and train our kids, but I think we've lost that this should be in a context of blessing and affirmation. When we have an atmosphere of unconditional love and speaking the best over our children, we put discipline and consequences in their proper context.

Whenever our children struggle, or we are facing something in our marriage or church, we pray blessing over one another and call out the truth of the Scripture we each need to hear.

Developing a regular habit of family meals increases a culture of

---

8. Proverbs 18:21a

blessing. Sadly, many families are not prioritizing meals around the table. With a strong culture of fun and blessing around the family table, you will have a stronger family altar.

> **May our spouse and children get the best of us, not the rest of us.**

My old youth pastor and mentor, Russ Babcock, used to tell me and other parents that if you only use directional and correctional speech with your kids, you don't really have a relationship with them.

The family table at our house is loud, fun, full of stories and full of laughter. I get it that life can be busy, but this is something that can be worked into a regular family habit.

We ought to pay the greatest attention to the circle of influence we have the greatest impact upon, and that place is the home. May God use us to change the world for Jesus, but not at the expense of our marriages and families. May our spouse and children get the best of us, not the rest of us.

If the people who love and respect me the most are the furthest from me, and I have no love or respect from my own family, I'm not successful in the eyes of God.

The greatest power to change the world doesn't start in board rooms or even prayer rooms, but in the bedrooms right down the hallway in my own home.

The Redeemed Family

Sometimes talk of family brings up more regrets and hurts than it does hope. Broken families have passed down broken systems from generation to generation. In some ways, even in the best of families, we are still affected by the brokenness of sin.

There are no perfect families.

The wonderful thing about God, though, is that He is a God of redemption. You might not have the perfect family, but you can have a redeemed family.

Even as we looked previously at Abraham, Isaac, Jacob and Gideon, we see family histories that are full of brokenness, selfishness and idolatry. But God's redemptive grace is available as we seek Him at the altar, even seeking Him for wisdom on how to repair a broken family altar.

Seek God in faith that He would give you wisdom about how to pray for your children if they are grown and have forsaken their faith. Seek God about how you might bless your children and grandchildren.

Maybe that's hard to conceive of right now in your family dynamics and circumstances, but God specializes in doing the impossible.

You might be the first in your family to break the curses of your generations. In Christ, God can give you a blessing to pass on that you never received from your natural family.

Find other Christians to pray with you for the turning of hearts toward one another in your family, and partner with the Holy Spirit in obedience as He leads you in your relationships.

Chapter 6

Restoring the Church Altar

"I've never seen it like this before."

In the last year or so of doing church together, my dad has said this to me several times.

I was raised in a church that has been a part of a move of God throughout the years in our region. My dad led the way in our region by developing a house of prayer, bringing pastors together in unity across denominations, and hosting conferences regularly on prayer, the prophetic and spiritual gifts.

But in this past year, the power of God has been breaking loose in our church in ways we haven't experienced in such a measure before. The spiritual hunger is almost tangible in our Sunday morning gatherings, and God encounters are increasing that lead people to deep repentance, deliverance from demonic oppression, spiritual and physical healing, as well as spiritual empowerment.

Through all the trials we faced in our church over the first five years of being lead pastors, our church has been renewed in our first love for Jesus.

First Love Fire

Jesus' test of first love was actually not for an individual believer in Revelation 2, but for the entire church of Ephesus. This Ephesian church that was birthed in a Holy Spirit revival under the apostle Paul's ministry, and then led by his spiritual son Timothy, did many things well.

Jesus commends this church for their deeds, their hard work, and their perseverance. He knows that they cannot tolerate wicked people, that they have tested those who claim to be apostles but are not, and have found them false. They have persevered and have endured hardships for His name, and have not grown weary."[1]

What a commendable list from Jesus. This apostolic hub was a multiplying church with the who's who of the ancient world attending like the apostle John at one time. But the rebuke from Jesus after His praise must have been a convicting blow, "Yet I hold this against you: You have forsaken the love you had at first. Consider how far you have fallen! Repent and do the things you did at first. If you do not repent, I will come to you and remove your lamp stand from its place."[2]

> **Church, we must repent if we have any other driving motivation in our churches that has usurped our loving allegiance to Jesus.**

It's like they were great at almost everything, but they forsook the one thing of loving Jesus first and most.

Not only are individual believer's lives examined by Jesus for faithfulness, but so are churches.

Jesus is looking for a community of believers who walk in simple

---

1. Revelation 2:2-3
2. Revelation 2:4-5

love and devotion to Him. Have we fallen in love with methods and programs? Are we going through the motions of rituals and practices without a heart fostering a deeper love for Jesus?

Church, we must repent if we have any other driving motivation in our churches that has usurped our loving allegiance to Jesus.

The church is the body of Christ, and Jesus is the head. We have one job ultimately, and that's to lift up the head. Just as Paul shared with us his apostolic burden to present each believer complete or mature in Christ, so he shares with us in Ephesians that God's plan for us collectively as the corporate church is also a maturity in Christlikeness. "'Instead, speaking the truth in love, we will grow to become in every respect the mature body of him who is the head, that is, Christ. From him the whole body, joined and held together by every supporting ligament, grows and builds itself up in love, as each part does its work."[3] We are to be in love with Jesus and to mature in that love to become like Him.

The church ought to be a community that cultivates the fire of first love at corporate altars.

Communion

One of the keys to restoring the altar in the church with a first love for Jesus is to make the table of the Lord central to our gatherings once again.

In communion or the Lord's supper we remember Christ's sacrifice on the altar for us. In Catholic, Anglican and other mainline churches, the altar is often in the center of the front of the sanctuary. The layout of churches historically puts the altar at the center of worship, or the holy place, which is a departure from the tabernacle of Moses. This is because the church adopted the pattern we see in heaven where the center of worship is the Lamb slain for us. The altar and the most holy place have become one in Christ. The pulpit for preaching and teaching is then off to the side. In the tradition of these placements, centrality is given to what Christ has done for us through the gospel, rather than to the preacher. While I don't believe it is necessary or binding to have this

---

3. Ephesians 4:15-16

arrangement physically in a church building, I believe it is necessary for us to recover a high honor for this holy meal.

Our church made the switch to take communion every week because it's part of historic Christianity, and we want to keep Jesus at the center of our services. We do a corporate reading from Scripture each week as we come to the table along with a reading from the Apostle's creed, the Nicene creed, the Didache or a declaration based on Biblical promises associated with Passover and communion. Each week seekers get to hear about what Christ has done through the gospel, see a physical representation of this truth, and observe Christians come to the altar to fellowship with Christ.

The word used throughout church history for this meal was the Eucharist which is based on the Greek word for thanksgiving. What is the gathering of the church if not a time for us to come together as the body of Christ to be thankful for what Jesus has done for us through His body broken?

Some Christians have more faith in encountering demons at the wrong table than encountering Christ at His table.

Paul said that we participate in, or fellowship with the body and blood of Jesus through the cup and the bread.[4]

This is in the context of warning about how we participate with demons at the altar or table of idols. Most Christians understand the negative power of opening up oneself to demons by fellowshiping with them through idolatry. Christians understand the warning to not be defiled by evil spirits, but sadly often believe that communion is just a symbolic exercise with no spiritual power.

Paul is teaching through correlation that by faith at the communion

---

4. 1 Corinthians 10:15-21

table, we fellowship with Christ through His body and blood. He is also correlating that where there is a negative connection to the presence of demons at idols' tables, there is also a positive connection to the presence of Jesus at His table. Some Christians have more faith in encountering demons at the wrong table than encountering Christ at His table.

How is this? It is a mystery.

When we take communion with thankfulness, reverence and awe, we release the power of Christ's presence in our church.

Dr. Randy Clark told me a story once about how he was ministering on the power of communion in a church that didn't have a high view of the Lord's supper. They did, however, have a high view of the anointing on a man of God.

During his sermon, people started walking to the altar and laying their coats and jackets at his feet. They wanted him to touch their clothes so that the anointing and impartation from his life would be released for miracles to them, as happened in the book of Acts. They had so much faith in the presence and power of God to be released through the laying on of hands and anointing oil, while believing that communion was just symbolic.

The Lord gave Randy an idea from Jesus' teaching on a prophet's reward. Jesus said, "Whoever welcomes a prophet as a prophet will receive a prophet's reward, and whoever welcomes a righteous person as a righteous person will receive a righteous person's reward."[5]

Randy asked the church, after sharing this Scripture, "If you receive a cracker as a cracker, what reward will you receive?"

"A cracker," they responded.

"If you receive grape juice as grape juice, what reward will you receive?"

"Grape juice," they responded again.

"Now if you receive the bread and the cup as the body and blood of Jesus, what reward will you receive?"

I think something clicked at this point.

Like Paul told the Corinthians, "For those who eat and drink

---

5. Matthew 10:41

without discerning the body of Christ eat and drink judgment on themselves."[6]

Randy was inviting the church to discern the body of Christ.

In 1 Corinthians 11 (and later in 12) we see a type of double meaning where the body of Christ means the sacrifice of Jesus' body, but also, the people who make the church. Paul told them to give more discernment to what they were actually receiving in the body and blood of Christ, and to gauge the health of other relationships in the church. Paul said that the judgment they brought on themselves is that people were sick and dying prematurely.

The Bible doesn't tell us how these elements are the body and blood of Jesus, but when we receive them, and discern them as Jesus said, there is supernatural power and fellowship with Him in His manifest presence.

Altar Calls

In Pentecostal churches, which I have been a part of my whole life, the altar call is central to our worship gatherings.

Charles Finney popularized altar calls in the Second Great Awakening. Other evangelists continued the trend throughout the decades. They mostly focused on a response to surrender to Christ as Lord and Savior. Other aspects of altar calls involved coming forward to publicly acknowledge and confess sins or specific responses to calls for obedience to Christ.

I hear they are not as in vogue, even in Pentecostal or Charismatic churches, as they once were. People are concerned that altar calls are based more on emotion and hype than on reasoned responses of obedience to God. There doesn't seem to be a clear pattern in Scripture for altar calls.

But Christian worship was also being developed during the time of the New Testament writings, and mostly happened in homes. We may not see specific altar calls, but we see space was given for people to approach Jesus and church leaders to declare their allegiance, and to

---

6. 1 Corinthians 11:29

receive prayer and ministry. Jesus almost always had someone do something like pick up their mat and walk or ask Him for something specifically to receive a miracle.

The principle of the altar call is making a place for people to connect with God.

Where I don't believe hype should motivate people, I also don't think that emotional decisions are always hype based. Most people's life changing moments with God involve some type of emotion or even intense emotion.

There should be no manipulation of emotions from preachers and leaders, but we must give space to people meeting Jesus in whole hearted devotion. From the earliest Bible stories, until today, the altar is simply a space we set aside to meet with God.

I believe churches should meet in homes, but I also believe churches should build buildings for public and corporate worship. Church buildings are outposts for the kingdom of God. They can become like a museum or even a funeral home of past moves of God, but they can also be a place where altars are established in cities and regions to connect Earth with heaven like altars of old.

I realize the people of the church are the body of Christ, and the people of the church are the temple of the Holy Spirit. But making a physical space where we model this and experience God together is a holy endeavor.

Lives are changed at the altar through communion and coming forward to meet with God.

Each week that I preach, I call people to the altar to repent of their sins, give their lives to Jesus, receive prayer for healing, deliverance, and personal needs. We used to have smaller responses, but I started inviting the church to pray for "a packed house, packed altars and packed hearts with the glory of God."

Space and time fail me to tell you about the lives that have been radically changed as people come to meet Jesus at the altar. In this space we have set aside as sacred for encountering the Lord, people regularly confess their sins with a depth of transparency and urgency.

People are freed from demonic oppression.

People are receiving the Holy Spirit.

Healing miracles are taking place.

Altar calls also make room practically for ministry to the church body (1 Corinthians 12) where spiritual gifts are expressed, and others are built up through prophecy, words of wisdom, words of knowledge, healings and miracles. The ministry of spiritual gifts fosters Christlike love between believers and blesses both the giver and receiver of ministry.

Having altar calls reinforces our expectation of God meeting us when we draw near to Him. Altar calls become a practical work to express our faith.

The Christian life should not be lived from altar call to altar call. We can't expect all of someone's spiritual formation to take place with outward responses. However, the testimonies of those who have encountered God at altars, have had life-changing experiences with Christ and been commissioned by the Holy Spirit to a life of fruitful mission, demand an examination for how we might incorporate these calls into the life of our churches.

Repentance and Confession

The church altar will not be restored without the church walking in repentance over sin.

The call to follow Jesus is a call to be separate from sin. "The Lord knows those who are his," and, "Everyone who confesses the name of the Lord must turn away from wickedness."'[7]

Many Pentecostal and Charismatic churches have turned away from the practice of confessing sin. Christians are being taught to confess their identity in Christ, but often at the expense of hiding the areas they are still struggling with in sin.

We need the gift of tears to flow in the church once again. We need to see and hear the cries of God's people to be free from besetting sin and come into agreement with God. It is a beautiful thing for men and women of God with their hands outstretched and hearts raised up to weep before the Lord over their own sin and the sins of their people.

---

7. 2 Timothy 2:19

"Godly sorrow brings repentance that leads to salvation and leaves no regret, but worldly sorrow brings death."[8]

Repentance or turning from sin begins with confession.

Public confession can be done in healthy and unhealthy ways. Sometimes public confession of sin inspires a spirit of repentance in a room and is historically a powerful part of revivals in the past.

To restore the altar in the church, however, we need to make space for repentance again, whether it is in front of a crowd or one on one with a minister or fellow Christian.

What we do with our sin matters.

Of course, we can confess it to God through Christ, but we must recover the instructions of confessing our sins to one another.

"Therefore confess your sins to each other and pray for each other so that you may be healed. The prayer of a righteous person is powerful and effective."[9]

"But if we walk in the light, as he is in the light, we have fellowship with one another, and the blood of Jesus, his Son, purifies us from all sin. If we claim to be without sin, we deceive ourselves and the truth is not in us. If we confess our sins, he is faithful and just and will forgive us our sins and purify us from all unrighteousness."[10]

The historic church made a regular place for Christians to confess sins and examine their lives.

The Methodists did this well under John Wesley and were organized into groups called class meetings, bands and holy clubs to confess sins to each other and help one another overcome in a spirit of love.

"Above all, love each other deeply, because love covers over a multitude of sins."[11]

I believe we need a return to the ancient practice of examining ourselves for repentance and confession like Wesley's holy club did with his *22 Questions* (See Appendix).

Repentance and confession will stoke the fires of revival in our

---

8. 2 Corinthians 7:10
9. James 5:16
10. 1 John 1:7-9
11. 1 Peter 4:8

hearts, our homes, and our churches. These things must be done both before the Lord and one another. We need to be a judgment free zone so that people are not further shamed while confessing their sin, while maintaining a spirit of no compromise when it comes to sin.

This should be modeled by healthy pastors and church leaders.

Let us resolve to live a life without secrets. Not everyone needs to know about our personal struggles, but we must be faithful to let God and other trusted people into our interior lives so that we walk in the holy light and love of Christ.

Gospel Preaching

Restoring the church altar will not be sustained without true gospel preaching. As a preacher, I mostly preach series exegetically from the Bible, always pointing to Jesus because the Book is all about Him. Often when people choose our church, they tell me, "You preach the Bible here."

I know there are many other churches faithfully preaching the gospel through the Scriptures, but the average Christian seeking a home church seems to think that sermons across the pulpits of today are filled with stories and inspirational thoughts but lack Biblical substance.

Charles Spurgeon once said, "I take my text and make a bee-line for the cross."[12]

Spurgeon was nicknamed the prince of preachers.

My Dad would often tell me a story about a man who invited his friend to go hear Charles Spurgeon preach. On their way home, the man asked his friend, "What did you think of the prince?"

His friend responded, "Oh, I met Him."

The man said, "You met Charles Spurgeon?"

He responded, "Who is that?"

His friend didn't know the prince of preachers, he was introduced to the Prince of Peace, Jesus Christ.

---

12. "https://credomag.com/2023/01/did-i-preach-christ/#:~:text=Charles%20Spurgeon%20once%20famously%20stated,this%20is%20a%20good%20desire.

Great preaching puts the preacher in the background and Jesus in the foreground.

My friend once attended a conference for preachers, and R.T. Kendall got up and told them, "Preach the blood or turn your badge in."

There is ultimately one message to preach, and the message is Jesus: His life, His death, His burial, His resurrection and His return, according to the Scriptures. I am not implying that we have such a narrow view of Scripture that we can't preach on marriage, prayer, obedience, etc. But all that we preach ought to be in light of the gospel.

The gospel is about preaching the message that brings true revival power and causes people to believe upon Christ, forsake sin and live a life of obedience by God's grace. I learned from Fleming Rutledge's lectures that true gospel preaching always ends with promise.

Christianity is about what God has done for us through Christ. We call Christians and sinners to obedience and various actions, but it should always be through the redemptive power of what God offers us through gospel promise.

I hear from people over and over again that when I preach, I am strong against sin and say hard things, but there is so much hope that people are drawn towards Christ, knowing that if they come to Him in repentance, He will accept them.

Gospel preaching that's all about Jesus will increase faith, repentance and the miraculous work of the Spirit. There is no true revival at the altars of our churches without uncompromised gospel preaching that points to the hope and grace we have in Jesus Christ.

Expressive Worship

The altar of a church is a place to lavish our love on Jesus together. The church and the people of God regularly gathered throughout history to encounter God in worship.

"You also, like living stones, are being built into a spiritual house to be a holy priesthood, offering spiritual sacrifices acceptable to God through Jesus Christ."[13]

We exist together corporately as the church and as individual believers to be a royal priesthood who worship God with spiritual praise.

Different traditions in the church and different cultures around the world have unique styles and methods of praising God. There is beauty in the diverse expressions and different parts of church worship. What's important is not that we worship the same way, but that we worship with the same Spirit. "Yet a time is coming and has now come when the true worshipers will worship the Father in the Spirit and in truth, for they are the kind of worshipers the Father seeks. God is spirit, and his worshipers must worship in the Spirit and in truth.""[14]

All throughout the Bible, we see pictures of worship being expressive with hands raised, people bowing down, singing, dancing and shouting. Even a word study on Hebrew and Greek words will show that when we see a word in English like "worship" or "praise" there is often a deeper understanding that accompanies these physical practices attached to the worship of our heart.

The church who wants a fire on the altar will bring God wholehearted and embodied praise, seeing their ministry as not to people first, but to the Lord first. After all, a priest's primary job is to minister to the Lord for the people.

We as a royal priesthood minister first and most to God to keep a fire burning in our churches. Singing in church shouldn't be hurried, it's not a mere preparation for the sermon but an act of worship that honors God. Jesus was moved by the costly worship of Mary of Bethany. We need to leave room for the people of God to bring extravagant and expressive praise to Jesus.

---

13. 1 Peter 2:5
14. John 4:23-24

A House of Prayer

One of my mentors in the faith and in ministry, Dr. Matthew K. Thomas from India, often told me, "If you want to find out how famous the guest speaker is, attend the conference. If you want to find out how famous the pastor is, attend the Sunday service. If you want to find out how famous Jesus is, attend the prayer meeting."

Very often we hear of the church rightly being referred to as the people of God, the family of God, the house of God, the body of Christ and the bride of Christ. However, we don't often hear the church being referred to as a house of prayer.

> Revival and spiritual awakening are dependent upon the church praying fervently for the salvation of the lost in our neighborhoods and in the nations of the earth.

Jesus said, "Is it not written: 'My house will be called a house of prayer for all nations'? But you have made it 'a den of robbers.'"[15]

Jesus said that His house, the church, is a house of prayer. These Scriptures Jesus is quoting from in the temple are from Jeremiah and Isaiah. Jesus came to observe the temple activity, and it grieved Him. He was righteously angry and drove merchants out of the temple; they had filled the courts of the Gentiles with money profiting schemes that added burdens to those coming to worship. The Gentiles wouldn't be able to come near as easily and hear about the One true God.

This is what Jesus said fulfilled what Jeremiah prophesied about "the den of robbers."

When Jesus referred to Isaiah's prophecy about the house of prayer,

---

15. Mark 11:17

He was also referring to a promise about His heart for the Gentile nations. "These I will bring to my holy mountain and give them joy in my house of prayer. Their burnt offerings and sacrifices will be accepted on my altar; for my house will be called a house of prayer for all nations.""[16] Here, God promises He will make us joyful in prayer, and that our prayers for all nations will lead to the nations coming to Him.

The prayer ministry of the church will have the largest impact on whether fire is burning on the altar. It's scary to me that churches can exist without any or very little prayer ministry. We want to see great awakening, but it will not come without the discipline and dedication of regular heartfelt prayer.

Jesus said that joyful prayer in His house will lead to the nations coming to Him. Prayer is not just a focus on our needs, but it is ultimately to pray for the advancement of the gospel to bring all nations to Jesus. Revival and spiritual awakening are dependent upon the church praying fervently for the salvation of the lost in our neighborhoods and in the nations of the earth.

Throughout the book of Acts, we see that the fire of a praying church caused the church to burn brightly in her mission rather than burn out. In...

- Acts 1 - The apostles and 120 total believers wait on the Lord in prayer for the promise of the Spirit.
- Acts 2 - While the 120 are waiting on God in prayer, the Holy Spirit supernaturally births the church in power and the three thousand new believers on that day continue to pray daily.
- Acts 3 - On Peter and John's walk to the hour of prayer, they heal the lame man at the gate, Beautiful.
- Acts 4 - When persecution rises, the church prays boldly, is filled with the Spirit again, and the place where they pray is shaken.

---

16. Isaiah 56:7

- Acts 6 - The apostles must appoint deacons to serve so they won't neglect the ministry of the Word and prayer.
- Acts 9 - Ananias is told Saul is praying while blind and in those days of blindness his eyes were truly opened to the supremacy of Jesus and the call on his life to suffer for the gospel.
- Acts 10 - Cornelius is a praying, God-fearing man, but not saved yet; yet his prayers are heard. Peter goes to pray on the rooftop and God supernaturally brings two praying men together to open up the gospel and the gift of the Holy Spirit to the Gentiles.
- Acts 12 - Peter escapes supernaturally from prison because of the prayers of the church.
- Acts 13 - Barnabas and Paul are set apart by the church to do the apostolic work of missions and church planting by a praying and fasting Antioch church.
- Acts 14 - Paul and Barnabas appointed elders wherever they went by prayer and fasting.
- Acts 16 - Paul and Silas are imprisoned because on their way to prayer, they are confronted by a demon possessed fortune teller, but by prayer and praise at the midnight hour, they get supernaturally delivered from prison and lead the Philippian jailer and his whole household to Christ.
- Acts 20 - Paul's final act of goodbye with the Ephesian elders was prayer following the great Asia minor revival that spread through his ministry.
- Acts 21 - Paul and his companions continue in prayer on a beach to sustain them on the journey between nations and cities.

We can have all the best programs and strategies, but if we want to be a part of true revival and awakening, we must get back to the way the church prayed at her genesis. It's time to return to the prayer meeting. It's time to rebuild the altar in our churches. Regular prayer is necessary for the ministry of the church to keep the fire burning of purity and power.

Chapter 7

The Altar of the Region

In 1749, the pastor and revivalist Jonathan Edwards wrote a book with the following title; *A Humble Attempt to Promote Explicit Agreement and Visible Union of All God's People in Extraordinary Prayer for a Revival of Religion and the Advancement of Christ's Kingdom on Earth.*

Pay attention to these keywords: "Explicit Agreement," "Visible Union," and "Extraordinary Prayer."

Edwards knew that revival and awakening would come as Christians and churches had unity in prayer through explicit agreement, came together publicly in visible union and prayed fervently with extraordinary prayer.

As I heard Jon Tyson describe Duncan Campbell's four altars that must be restored to bring revival to a region, my heart leapt with joy. I had already outlined the necessity of revival in the heart, the home and the church, but had not clearly yet articulated the call to pray as a region. We can have the altar of our heart, home and church burning, but we will miss out on the fullness of what God wants to do if we neglect corporate unity across our region.

The City Church

"I'll give you a vision that's as small as a city and as big as a soul."

I felt that phrase resound in my spirit as I was in prayer one day. I really felt that the Lord whispered this phrase to my heart. He was saying He wanted me to have a vision that, on the smallest scale, encompasses reaching a city, while also valuing how big it is to reach one soul.

We need to dream and have a vision of reaching entire cities and regions. It's not enough to have just one local growing church in a city. We need the church of a region to thrive.

I pastor in one of the least churched areas in the USA. As a youth pastor years ago, I belonged to a youth pastor network under Brian Muchmore's leadership. At our monthly lunches, Brian used to say, "If all of our youth groups doubled, the devil would still have the biggest youth group."

I got the message. We needed to work together and not compete if we were going to actually make a dent in Satan's kingdom.

When John wrote the words of Jesus in chapters 2 and 3 of Revelation, he wrote to seven city churches. Paul's letters were written to cities like Ephesus, Thessalonica and Corinth, but also to regions like Galatia. The churches in the cities of the New Testament times were a network of house churches.

People belonged to a local expression of the church that was led by elders and deacons. There are some references in the New Testament to specific house churches, but overall, the references to the church are local and universal.

The church was local, but the church was all one church. There were no denominations.

There were leadership troubles, moral failures and scandals that occurred, but they were ultimately all a part of the same church.

The word "catholic" was not first used as a denomination of the Western church, it referred to the whole universal church of all Christians. The one church on earth, the entire number of all Christians, will in the future be in heaven, the one bride of Christ for eternity.

The Biblical letters show us that God was examining the church from city to city. Maybe it's not enough to just be concerned about our own tribe, but to care for the health of the church across our city or county.

The Commanded Blessing

"Behold, how good and how pleasant it is for brethren to dwell together in unity! It is like the precious oil upon the head, Running down on the beard, The beard of Aaron, Running down on the edge of his garments. It is like the dew of Hermon, descending upon the mountains of Zion; For there the Lord commanded the blessing— Life forevermore."[1] What a promise from the Lord! The place where we dwell in unity is the place where God anoints us with His holy oil and commands a blessing!

One thing I know about doing ministry is that it is both incredibly taxing and amazingly glorious. I've been through enough seasons of battles and weariness to know I don't want to go it alone in my own strength or efforts. I long for the anointing of God on our church and ministry.

That's what we need in our churches right now: the commanded blessing of the Lord!

The anointing oil in the Bible was used to set things apart for God's purpose and represents the power of the Holy Spirit upon that which is anointed. Prophets, priests, and kings were anointed for their service. Items used for worship in the tabernacle were also consecrated with anointing oil.

If the Lord says He pours out oil on a unified people, get unified. Throughout Scripture, we see His anointing brings His favor, His blessing, His resourcing, His power, His deliverance, His healing, His protec-

---

1. Psalms 133:1-3 NKJV

tion, and His miracles. Not only do we get anointed when we come together in unity, He commands His blessing to be upon us.

Let the weight of that sink in.

God commanded the universe into existence.

God commands our obedience to His ways.

But those aren't the only commands He makes. He commands blessing to come upon His people who come together in unified agreement and oneness. That's what we need in our churches right now: the commanded blessing of the Lord!

The Prayer of Jesus

Jesus prayed what some call His High Priestly prayer in John 17. Jesus was praying for His disciples and for all future disciples. He is praying for us the most beautiful and powerful prayers as His hour of suffering was drawing near right before He went to the cross. "I do not pray for these alone, but also for those who will believe in Me through their word; that they all may be one, as You, Father, are in Me, and I in You; that they also may be one in Us, that the world may believe that You sent Me. And the glory which You gave Me I have given them, that they may be one just as We are one: I in them, and You in Me; that they may be made perfect in one, and that the world may know that You have sent Me, and have loved them as You have loved Me."[2]

Jesus prays for us to become one.

This is powerful language that goes beyond mere superficial unity. Jesus is praying that all of us would be one as He and the Father are one. Jesus is praying that the global church of all Christians would enter into oneness that He and the Father share. We are invited together into the oneness of our Triune God.

God has invited us to fellowship and participate with the love that the Father and Son share as one. We are to be as undivided as the Father and Jesus.

Christian oneness and unity scares a lot of Christians because we have created such barriers through all our church schisms and splits

---

2. John 17:20-23 NKJV

throughout history. Until 1054 AD, all the Christians were a part of the same church without denominations (there were certainly fractures of relationships and plenty of disunity before 1054, but no denominational differences).

In 1054, the church of the West, which became the Roman Catholic Church, and the church of the East, which became the Eastern Orthodox Church, excommunicated one another and cursed one another as both leaving the false church. The continued church splits that took place in the West take up volumes of church history books to see how we got Lutheran, Presbyterian, Baptist and other Protestant denominations.

We are invited together into the oneness of our Triune God.

The Eastern church splits are not as prominent in their history but there are certainly differences within the Eastern Orthodox churches and the divisions with Coptic, Syriac and Oriental Orthodox churches.

Catholic, Orthodox and Protestant denominations are all skeptical of others and quick to call each other heretics. How God would bring us all back together and make us one would be one of the greatest miracles in history.

But of course, with God, all things are possible.

Christians, we need to return to the prayer and heart of our Lord in John 17 and pray in agreement with Him. How can we call ourselves Christians, literally "little-Christ's," if we do not pursue the same heart as Jesus.

We must live a lifestyle of loving and honoring one another. Jesus said, "By this everyone will know that you are my disciples, if you love one another."[3] This is the way.

---

3. John 13:35

I have a shirttail relative who I have only met twice, named Chase Jarvis. Chase is a world-famous photographer and videographer. He's done photos and videos for some of the largest companies in the world. His work is beautiful, and he has launched other businesses around creativity, marketing and business. What made Chase unique in the photography world was when he first started in his career, he went online and posted how he got the unique shots he was taking. He listed his gear, his settings, and the details necessary to help other people get similar pictures. This wasn't normal in his industry because he was giving away the secrets to his success. But Chase quoted the old aphorism when he shared about this, "A rising tide lifts all boats."

His perspective was that if he helped others innovate and advance the art, he would learn from them and everyone would get better.

I wish we saw this in the church more and I'm hopeful with the rising leaders in this generation.

My friend Ben Dixon pastors in the Pacific Northwest, and for years, has run a ministry to help the church with discipleship and the development of spiritual gifts. He used to run a conference each year called *Continuing the Ministry of Jesus*.

Grace and I along with a team were running a conference called *Represent*.

Ben called me one day and said that he wanted to lay down his conference to support mine. He believed we could reach more people and be more effective if we worked together. It was humbling to have a friend be selfless like that.

For many years, we saw hundreds and thousands of people come together to be equipped in lifestyle and power evangelism through our conferences. It wouldn't have happened to the same degree if we were on our own.

My Dad united pastors for many years with a monthly prayer luncheon and united nights of worship throughout our county and region. Pastors came and encouraged one another, wept together and prayed together. Occasionally, they would rent a civic hall out and fill it with worshippers from dozens of churches and denominations. The group even organized a community service day to bless one of our local cities and save the city thousands of dollars.

I'm seeing an increase of prayer meetings and pastors longing to gather again in our local region. Pastor Sean Gasperetti partners with me in Everett to host pastors across Snohomish County for monthly prayer. In this past year, the hunger in pastors has been unusually strong to get to prayer.

We make the same pitch, but we are getting a different response. It feels like the beginning of something bigger than what any of us can make happen on our own.

Time will tell.

But these meetings of prayer are marked with fervency and expectation of God working in our city. As I've heard it said, we gather, "without egos, logos or labels."

Pastors coming together are from mega-churches, small churches, and Christian non-profit ministries. No one is there flexing about how their thing is better. We just unify and come around the person of Christ to be exalted so that our region might know Him.

I'm hearing reports from Bishop Joseph Mattera of prayer networks re-emerging in the Northeast in New York and other cities. When I was growing up in the 90s and early 2000s, I remember more prayer networks and large gatherings for Christians. I'm encouraged to hear of *America Prays, Intercessors for America, David's Tent, Contend Global,* the *Send* and many other movements that are mobilizing for prayer and mission.

We need a type of unity that goes beyond performance or special events. We must retain faithfulness to the historic faith that was "once for all delivered to the saints."[4] I'm not calling for a fake unity or us gathering around different gospels or false gods. We must hold to the essential doctrines of Christ and the Scriptures. But we must prefer one another and invest in one another's success. We need to pray for one another, give to one another, weep with one another, and rejoice with one another. We need to pray and work to be one as Jesus prays for us to be one.

---

4. Jude 1:3b NKJV

The Power of Praying Together

I believe the best way to rebuild an altar in our region is to get the church praying together. Something happens in an atmosphere of prayer; the Holy Spirit works beyond our best strategies. Praying with brothers and sisters from different tribes and streams in the body of Christ is the key to uniting. God does things sovereignly as we posture ourselves in humility and cry out to Him together.

We have too much pride.

We like things our own way.

We have our theological distinctives.

We have our own churches and lives to worry about.

It's only through yielding in prayer to the Holy Spirit that He can bring us together and cause us to be united for His purposes.

In Acts 4, after pressure and persecution, the church's first response is to pray. They don't see trouble as a sign of God's displeasure, but they let it unite them and lift up their voices boldly. They saw opposition as an opportunity to pray and see a move of God.

As they prayed for power and boldness this is how God responded, "After they prayed, the place where they were meeting was shaken. And they were all filled with the Holy Spirit and spoke the word of God boldly."[5]

> **When we come together in unity, the Spirit moves. When the Spirit moves, He brings us into a deeper unity.**

They couldn't have cued the earth shaking and the outpouring of the Spirit, but they could posture themselves in a united attitude in prayer. They prayed together in agreement and God does things that are

---

5. Acts 4:31

beyond our best efforts in prayer. When we come together in unity, the Spirit moves. When the Spirit moves, He brings us into a deeper unity.

> **May we quit trying to gain the glory for ourselves, when Jesus has already given it to us to bring us together in oneness.**

I've seen over and over how prayer and a move of the Spirit brings the generations together. In the early 1900s, at the Azusa Street revival, the atmosphere of prayer and unity brought down walls between races.

If we would get together for simple unity around the glory and mission of Jesus Christ, God will do things beyond our best abilities. A united church walking in oneness across our regions will draw the commanded blessing of the Lord upon us.

We are so often looking for the glory, but Jesus told us in His high priestly prayer that He has already given us His glory so that this may be accomplished.

May we quit trying to gain the glory for ourselves, when Jesus has already given it to us to bring us together in oneness.

CHAPTER 8

How do we Really Change the World?

In 1975, Loren Cunningham, the founder of *YWAM*, and Bill Bright, the founder of *Campus Crusade for Christ*, shared with one another a similar vision they had received in prayer of Christians reaching the seven mountains of influence. This became known as the Seven Mountain Mandate.

The Seven Mountains are these areas of culture: Religion, Family, Education, Government, Media, Arts and Entertainment, and Business. These ideas really started to gain traction in Pentecostal and Charismatic circles in the 2010s, especially around churches that are labeled as being a part of the New Apostolic Reformation (NAR).

Cunningham and Bright were not the first to emphasize these types of ideas of how Christianity might permeate culture and influence society with her values. I believe Abraham Kuyper, the Dutch theologian and politician, had more depth and clarity than a lot of what we see in today's Seven Mountain teachings. Kuyper referred to the areas of culture as spheres. This is a better framework.

Nowadays, I've heard people referring to Seven Mountain doctrines and prophecies. As a mission strategy, it's necessary for Christians to engage in every area of culture. What some of these interpretations and applications of the Seven Mountain Mandate have turned into has become either wacky practices or counterproductive actions to the actual mission of Jesus. Christians are convinced they need to rule from mountains to control culture in order to fulfill the great commission.

This comes at a time where it not only has affected the mission of the Pentecostal and charismatic types, but many Reformed Christians have embraced an extreme Christian nationalist vision of the church dominating American government and enforcing a theocracy with imprisonment and executions for those who don't fall in line. If you read church history, you see we don't do well when we have all the power and authority.

Christian values and ideas that are rooted in the Scriptures will create the best world for us to live in before Christ returns. There is nothing wrong with influencing our culture through Christians in art, science, business and education. And if godly Christians lead areas of culture, it's a beautiful thing.

> **The kingdom advances through altars, those who lay down their lives like Jesus. Our calling to stand up for Christ never eclipses our calling to be like Christ.**

I would prefer a Christian society to a godless, secular society. But the issue is when we resort to exerting our influence through power and control. We Christians could rule all the kingdoms of the world and still have it wrong because "Jesus said, "My kingdom is not of this world. If it were, my servants would fight to prevent my arrest by the Jewish leaders. But now my kingdom is from another place.""[1]

The problem is that we can sit on thrones of influence, but the kingdom is not brokered by those who have wealth, power and status.

The kingdom advances through altars, those who lay down their

---

1. John 18:36

lives like Jesus. Our calling to stand up for Christ never eclipses our calling to be like Christ.

Do Thrones Matter?

This book might make it sound like I think leaders in government and business don't matter. So, I want to correct that potential fallout from the tone of my writing. Thrones do matter to God, and they do matter in human history for the purposes of God.

God still cares about the destiny of nations. He will judge nations and rulers. In Psalm 2, which is the second most quoted Psalm in the New Testament, the Psalmist writes a prophetic Psalm about God's dealings with nations and their leaders.

"Therefore, you kings, be wise; be warned, you rulers of the earth. Serve the Lord with fear and celebrate his rule with trembling. Kiss his son, or he will be angry and your way will lead to your destruction, for his wrath can flare up in a moment. Blessed are all who take refuge in him."[2]

The primary issue of world leaders when it comes to God's judgements is how they value and submit to Christ. Psalm 2 declares that God laughs at His enemies when He hears their schemes. He is not afraid or caught off guard by the plotting of evil rulers.

God actually desires good government that allows the gospel message to flourish in a culture. We see this in Paul's writing to Timothy about the importance of praying for leaders who occupy thrones.

"I urge, then, first of all, that petitions, prayers, intercession and thanksgiving be made for all people— for kings and all those in authority, that we may live peaceful and quiet lives in all godliness and holiness. This is good, and pleases God our Savior, who wants all people to be saved and to come to a knowledge of the truth. For there is one God and one mediator between God and mankind, the man Christ Jesus, who gave himself as a ransom for all people. This has now been witnessed to at the proper time."[3]

---

2. Psalms 2:10-12
3. 1 Timothy 2:1-6

Prayer altars have the power to affect thrones. We should especially pray for those who lead from thrones of power and influence.

> **Prayer altars have the power to affect thrones. We should especially pray for those who lead from thrones of power and influence.**

Our prayers are to be aimed at a culture that allows us to live peaceful and quiet lives in all godliness and holiness.

Why?

Because Paul says this creates an environment for people to be saved as the church freely does her ministry. God doesn't want anyone to perish. So, prayer altars affect those on the thrones and those on the thrones can help create an environment that allows prayer altars to flourish. We ought to vote when we have the right to, as we pray, for a good government that allows gospel ministry to prosper.

We have mixed things up when we put more faith in thrones or think Christians must occupy thrones to change the world and bring spiritual awakening. God appoints government leaders who "do not bear the sword for no reason. They are God's servants, agents of wrath to bring punishment on the wrongdoer."[4] The job of those on thrones as they are appointed by God, is to punish evil and reward good. They are supposed to keep a just and peaceful society in order.

The government cannot bring about revival and spiritual awakening.

As Kuyper would see it, we need to respect sphere sovereignty. The church is not tasked with punishing evildoers and the government is not tasked with discipleship.

The spheres of culture influence one another, and they are all

---

4. Romans 13:4

accountable to Christ, but we must not lose faith in the altar to change the world.

The church and Christians throughout these seven spheres appeal to the world as salt and light to bring our influence, service, solutions and creativity as we point people to Jesus.[5] The government uses coercion and force to enact change by enforcing laws. The church brings change by the power of God and the way of Jesus.

> **Prayer altars affect those on the thrones and those on the thrones can help create an environment that allows prayer altars to flourish.**

In *Strange New World,* Carl R. Trueman does a masterful job at demonstrating how the collective worldview of Western Culture has been shaped through the centuries. One of the most surprising and outstanding insights that Trueman makes in that book is how Karl Marx and his communist ideals have succeeded in changing not only those who agree with his ideas, but even his opponents. Marx framed the world economically between the bourgeoisie and the proletariat, or between the haves and the have nots, the ruling class and the working class.

So how did Marx succeed at distorting all our thinking whether we agree with him or not? We tend to see everything as a money issue tied to power, so therefore, in this line of thinking, all solutions must be solved by the government. It's hard for us to even think of changing the world without having the "right" government create the "right" policies for the issues we care about the most.

A lot of the seven mountain influencers and teachers that I've heard in the past decade mostly emphasize the need to get certain people

---

5. Matthew 5:13-16

elected to government. They talk a little about other areas of culture, but it seems that the faith in the government throne has eclipsed them all. We need to conceptualize other methods of changing the world than solely winning elections and having political power.

Eighteenth-century Scottish patriot Andrew Fletcher said, "Let me make the songs of a nation, and I care not who makes its laws."[6]

This is someone who understands that to move the hearts of culture, there are other ways than government. Christians need to bring their influence to every area of culture so that we might reach people for Christ in every area of culture.

If we create Christian structures without Christlike people running the structures, the structures will crumble and fall. Christians ought to partner with God and write beautiful music, create compelling films, write the best novels, build innovative schools, develop state-of-the-art hospitals and solve global problems with cutting edge technologies.

We can touch the heart and soul of people in the world in a way that the government never can. So, the question is not should Christians go into every area of culture, but how should we go into every sphere, to build altars, or climb thrones?

> **The question is not should Christians go into every area of culture, but how should we go into every sphere, to build altars, or climb thrones?**

---

[6]. https://www.neh.gov/article/music-pa-ingalls-played#:~:text="Let%20me%20make%20the%20songs,Scotland%2C%20English%20political%20machinations%20notwithstanding.

The Real Unseen Power

There is a real unseen power to change the world in prayer.

I'm afraid that our focus on the Seven Mountains has caused many Christians to subconsciously lose faith in the power of prayer. I'm also afraid that many Christians on the extreme left and the extreme right have come to view prayer as inactivity.

Throughout the past several years of racial tensions and issues as well around our global health pandemic, I often heard secular influenced believers say things like, "Don't send me your thoughts and prayers."

The message was loud and clear. People don't think prayer is action. Sentiments from far-right Christian nationalists are not much better when it comes to piety and prayer. All that seems to matter is force and exerting Christian morals in the public square.

The apostle Paul gives us a look at our real but unseen power in prayer.

The ones pulling the strings of rulers and powers are not mere mortals or things we can observe in our physical universe. "Finally, be strong in the Lord and in his mighty power. Put on the full armor of God, so that you can take your stand against the devil's schemes. For our struggle is not against flesh and blood, but against the rulers, against the authorities, against the powers of this dark world and against the spiritual forces of evil in the heavenly realms."[7]

Here we see that we are wrestling against spiritual powers who try to control the world.

The Scriptures show us we are in a world at war. If we conceptualize problems outside of a spirit world and a spiritual war with God's kingdom against the kingdom of darkness, we are starting at a point that is unbiblical. When we try to change the world through thrones primarily and neglect prayer altars, it's like we are bringing a pea shooter to a nuclear war.

This is why even when great militaries and dictators have tried to wipe out Christianity, destroy churches and burn Bibles, they are ulti-

---

7. Ephesians 6:10-12

mately not successful because there is a spirit world in operation that even world leaders are underneath.

Christians who pray can change the world. We have the power of Elijah in our prayers. Power to affect a nation with more authority than earthly thrones.

"Elijah was a human being, even as we are. He prayed earnestly that it would not rain, and it did not rain on the land for three and a half years. Again he prayed, and the heavens gave rain, and the earth produced its crops."[8]

There is a power in the praying church that no earthly power can touch.

Fidelity to Christ

The altar is the way of Jesus to change the world. True change comes from Christ and His way of life. Thinking that power or occupying thrones is the main way to change the world is to think of the kingdom being of this world. Fidelity to Christ matters most when it comes to having a true influence in the world.

What if you create the best family policy but you leave your spouse?

What if you help donate to fight human trafficking but are personally addicted to pornography?

What if you assert that the government leaders you voted for are truly righteous, but behind the scenes, they are full of corruption for their own profits?

Can you see it?

We have to actually live out our faith personally and in every area of life while partnering with God in prayer to overcome the evil strategies with which Satan is attacking this world.

We need to put our faith in the altar, which is a relinquishing of our power and control to God. Faith in the altar is about a life of prayer that is ultimately not a faith in ourselves, but a faith in God. The church is not called so much to stand up for Jesus, but to stand up *like* Jesus.

This is the way of the martyrs and heroes of the faith who overcame

---

8. James 5:17-18

Satan and shaped history. "They triumphed over him by the blood of the Lamb and by the word of their testimony; they did not love their lives so much as to shrink from death."[9]

The way of Jesus and His apostles reshaped the world.

Historian Tom Holland wrote an entire best-selling book on this very truth, *Dominion: How the Christian Revolution Remade the World*. He writes about how Christianity has reshaped the values and virtues of the West and much of the world.

We take for granted things like love, faithfulness in marriage, the end of slavery, hospitals, women's rights and human rights. All these things which seem like a given in society came from the one who made beauty and meaning come out of suffering on the cross.

If we want to influence the world for Christ, ought not we influence the world like Christ? Jesus and His followers changed the world with a message, a way of life, and the reality of God's power.

History Makers and the Altar

"History belongs to the intercessors,"[10] said Walter Wink.

Who are the heroes of heaven? Those who ruled from thrones or those who laid down their lives on the altar? I'm not trying to imply that only martyrs make history, but those who give their all for God's purposes.

While thrones do matter and have great consequences according to who sits on them, the greatest power to change the world is the laid down life of the altar in prayer, obedience and being faithful to Christ even in suffering.

I think we often neglect the power of a life of prayer, consecration, and obedience. And when I say obedience, I mean obedience in a holistic sense, not just in our character, but also in our calling and purpose for vocation.

Taking care of your marriage, loving your family, participating in the

---

9. Revelation 12:11
10. https://www.goodreads.com/quotes/8333426-history-belongs-to-the-intercessors---those-who-believe-and

life of a church, working with your hands as unto the Lord, being prayerful, giving of your wealth and being faithful to God in the hidden areas of life have the power to preserve and shape the world around you.

As Christians, we understand we are supposed to pray and do good things, but can we really change history?

Many Christians throughout our history have shaped the world through art, science, theology, government, and philosophy. History is filled with men and women of God who lived lives of prayer, holiness, and obedience. Only heaven knows the true heroes of history.

> **We look back to see what may happen ahead if we pray, "God, do it again."**

In 203, Felicitas and Fortunata were sisters in Christ imprisoned for their faith in Carthage and sent to their death in an arena for the entertainment of the crowds.[11] They had a confident defiance in the face of death. Their lack of fear and expression of Christlike love towards one another and their fellow Christians at their martyrdom was a witness to the power of the altar, which led to many in the crowd being so disturbed they eventually converted to Christianity.

In the 400s, the Irish took Saint Patrick captive into slavery as a teenager, and eventually, he escaped when he was a young man. Through a spiritual vision, God called Patrick back to Ireland. Patrick used the power of prayer, creative gospel preaching and the working of miracles to convert the pagan Irish from witchcraft and idolatry to a vibrant faith in Jesus Christ. Much of Western culture was created and preserved by the work of Saint Patrick's followers.[12]

---

11. From the Patient Ferment of the Early Church by Alan Kreider
12. Pentecost to the Present, Book One: Early Prophetic and Spiritual Gift Movements by Jeff Oliver and the Celtic Way of Evangelism by George C. Hunter III

What began from a prayer altar changed a nation and impacted culture for centuries to come.

John Knox in the 1500s was a man who prayed a famous and aggressive prayer, "Give me Scotland or I die." He gave his life fully to the call of God in his generation. Mary Queen of Scots said of him, "I fear the prayers of John Knox more than all the assembled armies of Europe."

The altar shook the throne. Knox helped revive the ministers of Great Britain and helped influence the book of Common Prayer.[13]

The Moravian prayer movement was led by Count Nicolaus Ludwig von Zinzendorf in the 1700s, who was a wealthy landowner and a pietist Christian. He brought people who were persecuted from various people groups and denominations into an agreement of Christian unity. Through a movement of prayer, God birthed a global missions movement. They had 24 women and 24 men pray in one hour shifts for 24-7 prayer. This kind of prayer altar established 232 missions worldwide.[14]

John Wesley, in the 1700s, saw revival as he preached throughout England. He formed his followers into small groups called holy clubs, class meetings, and bands. His small groups transformed British society as people came together across upper and lower classes as equals to confess their sins and help each other overcome temptation. As lives changed at the altar of confession and Christian virtues, society was transformed.[15]

In Charles Finney's ministry in the 1800s, as captured in his autobiography, there is a direct impact between his life of prayer and revival. Finney saw whole cities impacted by the gospel. Father Nash was his main intercessor and when they prayed before his meetings, they saw astounding results and conversions to Christ.[16] God prepared cities, churches, and groups of people ahead of time, as Nash contended in prayer at the altar and then Finney would see the manifestation of the results as he preached the gospel.

---

13. https://learn.ligonier.org/articles/give-me-scotland-or-i-die
14. Pentecost to the Present, Book Two: Reformations and Awakenings by Jeff Oliver
15. John Wesley's Class Meetings by D. Michael Henderson
16. Autobiography of Charles G. Finney

William and Catherine Booth in the 1800s launched the Salvation Army.[17,18,19] They preached the gospel and helped the poor. Their movement was born out of the holiness movement. They had a focus on the gospel, repentance and prayer, but they added to it the importance of caring for the poor, the addict and the imprisoned. Their organization to this day is a world leader in aid and relief to the broken.

What started at the altar continues to shape the world with the love of Christ.

> **The church is not called so much to stand up for Jesus, but to stand up *like* Jesus.**

William Seymour, in the early 1900s, was a one eyed black preacher who led a revival that is still shaping world history today known as the Azusa Street Revival.[20] He endured mistreatment as a black man from white church leaders, but was so desperate for a move of God, he refused to be denied. The Spirit led him to Azusa Street, and he often hid his face in a box near the altar during the meetings. The Pentecostal movement was born, and it has become the fastest growing group within Christianity. Countless souls have been added to the kingdom of God, schools built, ministries to the poor started, churches planted and many nations blessed out of Seymour's ministry of prayer, preaching and obedience.

Rees Howells was a Welshman who was gripped with the call of God to pray in the late 1800s and 1900s. He saw the results of prayer and fasting throughout his life, as God gave him very specific assignments in prayer. His prayers led to salvations, healings and revivals throughout nations. Eventually, as he prayed over national and

---

17. https://en.wikipedia.org/wiki/William_Booth
18. https://en.wikipedia.org/wiki/Catherine_Booth
19. Pentecost to the Present, Book Two: Reformations and Awakenings by Jeff Oliver
20. https://revival-library.org/heroes/william-seymour/

international events, his prayers along with other intercessors impacted World War II as there are documented answers to prayer that affected the outcome of the battles for Dunkirk and Britain. His prayers were mightier than the sword, and his ministry at the altar defeated the extension of Hitler's throne.[21]

The altar has conquered many thrones throughout history. We must remember the heroes of faith throughout the generations. We need to read their stories and tell their testimonies. The heroes of heaven are not only those who are preachers, pastors and missionaries, but those who give their all for God wherever they are called. The Bible calls these heroes who gave it all those of "whom the world is not worthy."[22]

What has happened before must provoke in us a hunger to lay down our lives at the altar of prayer that God might do it again. We look back to see what may happen ahead if we pray, "God, do it again."

---

21. Rees Howells Intercessor by Norman Grubb
22. Hebrews 11:38

Chapter 9

True Prophets and the Altar

I grew up in a home and a church that has a great value for the prophetic ministry. My dad started hosting prophetic conferences before it was popular in the 90s. He faced persecution and criticism for doing so. I got to grow up in church enjoying the benefits of prophetic ministry without having to pay a price for it. I honor my parents for their obedience to God. I love and value the prophetic ministry.

While growing up around it, I saw my parents have very healthy safeguards for how they processed the prophetic and trained our church to do so. The prophetic has incredible power to direct people's lives, so we need to have accountability with that kind of power. The prophetic is only one of the gifts to the church and should never solely direct people's lives and faith.

Prophetic words should be tested and weighed according to the Scriptures. Prophetic words, even when confirmed and in alignment with Scripture, need great care in applying along with godly counsel, life circumstances, prayerful timing and the witness of the Holy Spirit.

As someone who has grown up virtually my entire life around the prophetic ministry, I am shocked by what has been exposed and demonstrated in the prophetic movement during the past several years of the charismatic and prophetic streams of the American church.

I have been trained my whole life to not think of prophets as infallible. Prophecy in Scripture is without error. Anything that God actually speaks prophetically is also without error. The error comes in our transmission and communication of what we are hearing and discerning as God's voice.

Paul teaches us about the importance and boundaries of prophecy, "Do not quench the Spirit. Do not treat prophecies with contempt but test them all; hold on to what is good, reject every kind of evil."[1]

Prophecy is important to the life of the church, the believer, and the activity of the spirit. But it must be tested. I started hearing from the same prophetic community that taught me to test prophecies and not expect perfection from prophets, doubling down on prophecies that were not coming to pass rather than respond to simple tests and apologize for not hearing clearly.

Critics of prophets neglect the fact that the Bible says prophecy is a spiritual gift, embracing novel interpretations that lead to cessationism. Critics of prophecy also neglect Scriptures like "For we know in part and we prophesy in part."[2]

Prophets only get glimpses of revealed facts and future possibilities for events. But this is why testing and judging is so important. The problem we run into now is not only from the critics or cessationists, but the prophets who believe that judging prophecies means you reject prophecy altogether.

I had people leave my church, watch other people judge one another wrongfully and break fellowship in the body of Christ over prophecies that were never fulfilled.

I've had multiple people tell me that by this time there would be invading armies in America waging war, the stock market would crash and there would be specific outcomes to our elections. I've had people confront me over government conspiracies that were supposedly exposed by prophets that had no basis in truth.

---

1. 1 Thessalonians 5:19-22
2. 1 Corinthians 13:9

When these prophecies have been shown to be false, and I do not agree with them, they act as if I am in the wrong. While I don't expect every prophet to have perfect accuracy, what do we do with prophets who are getting things wrong most of the time, or fail to admit they have missed it entirely, while people make life-altering decisions based on their prophetic words?

These words of Jesus are so sobering and convicting to me as a charismatic leader who loves the prophetic, "Not everyone who says to me, 'Lord, Lord,' will enter the kingdom of heaven, but only the one who does the will of my Father who is in heaven. Many will say to me on that day, 'Lord, Lord, did we not prophesy in your name and in your name drive out demons and in your name perform many miracles?' Then I will tell them plainly, 'I never knew you. Away from me, you evildoers!'"[3]

> **We need to see true prophets who protect the altar.**

Who are we kidding when we are covering up for these errors in our own movement and making excuses for the mishandling of the prophetic gifts? We might fool ourselves, but we will be the fool on judgement day if we don't repent and get in the right place as prophets of the Lord.

I say all this as someone who loves the prophetic ministry.

I am walking in fulfilled prophetic words over my life. My call to ministry was prophetic and confirmed through very specific circumstances. I've seen people get healed, delivered and saved through prophecy. I've watched specific prophetic words mobilize prayer and action in the church locally and nationally. We regularly have corporate and personal words given in our church and I will continue to honor

---

3. Matthew 7:21-23

prophecy and prophets, but we need to see purity restored to the prophetic.

We need to see true prophets who protect the altar.

Prediction or Purity

Depending on your church tradition, you probably see prophets as truth tellers who call the church to purity in righteousness and justice, or as those who see the secrets of human hearts and make prophetic predictions about future events before they happen.

True prophets in the Scripture do both, but I believe the word of the Lord for this season is for prophets to protect the purity of the altar over an allegiance to the power of thrones.

Reading the Biblical prophets, it is hard to substantiate the modern prophetic practice of choosing a political side and prophesying down a party line or with current fads or trends.

Prophets speak for God.

Their allegiance is to heaven.

They are speaking from heaven to earth, from God to humanity.

My dad likes to summarize the Angel of the Lord's message to Joshua before he leads the Israelites to take Jericho. Joshua asks Him, "Whose side are you on?"

The Lord basically says in response, "I don't come to take sides, I have come to take over."

I'm not calling for middle ground on moral and Biblical issues, I am talking about calling every side of the political spectrum into obedience to God.

In King David's life, there was a powerful prophet named Nathan. Nathan was a court prophet. The kings throughout Israel's history wanted prophets and wise counselors to help them with the problems they faced in their nation.

Nathan was a faithful prophet who not only respected the throne but was faithful to protect the altar, the purity of the ministry. Nathan encouraged David and was supportive of him as he followed God, but he was not so enamored with David that he avoided rebuking him and confronting David over his sin. When David committed adultery with

Bathsheba and had her husband Uriah killed to cover it all up, Nathan didn't ignore David's sin, he called him on it.

Accurate predictions in prophecy are not the highest test for true prophets. God warned Israel about prophets that could predict future events through visions and dreams accurately, but could also lead people astray. "If a prophet, or one who foretells by dreams, appears among you and announces to you a sign or wonder, and if the sign or wonder spoken of takes place, and the prophet says, "Let us follow other gods" (gods you have not known) "and let us worship them," you must not listen to the words of that prophet or dreamer. The Lord your God is testing you to find out whether you love him with all your heart and with all your soul."[4] True prophets will not lead people astray to false gods. The purity of the prophetic heart is more important to discern than the claims and signs of the prophet. Accuracy matters to the Lord, but it's not the most important characteristic of a true prophet.

In Ezekiel 12, 13 and 14, God is judging the prophets of Israel. In Ezekiel 12, God issued His judgements and says that they will not delay no matter what people prophesy by their own imaginations.

> **The prophet's true loyalty is to God and being faithful to His ways.**

God will judge prophets who make up things according to their own imaginations.

In Ezekiel 13, God issued His judgement against the people and the prophets for falsely prophesying peace when there is no peace. Prophets are not supposed to just tell people good news and tickle their ears with what they want to hear. God likens them to a false wall that looks good but is flimsy and easily destroyed.

In Ezekiel 14, God issued His judgement against the people for their

---

4. Deuteronomy 13:1-3

doublemindedness and compromised hearts to seek both prophets and idols. It's interesting to read this chapter because the people have replaced their love for inquiring of the Lord themselves, and they are relying upon the idols of false gods as well as relying on prophets to hear God for them. The Lord will not be replaced in our lives. He will not allow the altars of our heart or churches to replace our trust in Him with false teachings or even other prophetic voices.

Just when you think you have the prophetic ministry figured out, there is another story that is perplexing about how God deals with people through the prophetic. "Then a spirit came forward and stood before the Lord, and said, 'I will persuade him.' The Lord said to him, 'In what way?' So he said, 'I will go out and be a lying spirit in the mouth of all his prophets.' And the Lord said, 'You shall persuade him, and also prevail. Go out and do so.' Therefore look! The Lord has put a lying spirit in the mouth of all these prophets of yours, and the Lord has declared disaster against you."["][5]

This is one of the more bizarre realities of the prophetic. God can judge us by allowing a prophet to prophesy lies that we really want to hear. Not only do we see this happen in 1 Kings 22, In Jeremiah 5:31, God says, "the prophets prophesy lies… and my people love it this way."[6]

I've seen Christians run from prophet to prophet to try and get some kind of vague word that they might interpret in such a way that empowers their sinful lifestyle. If we refuse to submit to the simple and clear meaning of Scripture, and value prophecy above what we know to be right in God's eyes, God can give us a word that sounds like it is coming from Him, but is only what we want to hear. So even hearing something that feels confirming to us can actually be judgment against us if we refuse to have a heart that is submitted to God.

Christian, we need to be careful with the prophetic and not just use it when it serves what we want to hear for ourselves, our churches, our politics, or our nations. We need prophets who are loyal to God and church leaders that will test and weigh prophecies for their purity as well as their predictions.

---

5. I Kings 22:21-23 NKJV
6. Jeremiah 5:31

Prophets regularly called the people of God back to faithfulness to God and away from idolatry, immorality, and oppressing the poor. I will deal with this in the next chapter, but true prophets cared about the purity of worship among God's people and didn't ignore disobedience to keep a political agenda going. The prophet's true loyalty is to God and being faithful to His ways.

The Spirit of Prophecy

We see some common threads throughout the Old and New Testament prophets, but also some uniqueness between their ministries. Most importantly, both are called to be personally faithful to God and loyal to Him in their ministry above all else. But in the New Testament, we see there is something very important that prophets of our day cannot forsake and be a true prophet.

In Revelation, John hears this "For the testimony of Jesus is the spirit of prophecy.""[7]

Prophets who protect the purity of the altar in the New Covenant are ultimately faithful to one message, the testimony of Jesus. Some have applied, with some validity, the testimony of Jesus to mean anything Jesus does for one person, He can do again in someone else's life.

However, I think in the context of Revelation 19 we see a greater meta-truth that prophecy is ultimately to point to the supremacy of Christ and the sufficiency of what He has accomplished as the Lamb of God who was slain for us.

Prophecy that does not ultimately point to Jesus or the finished work of His death, burial, resurrection, and return is not the spirit of prophecy. Prophets can predict events, call out people's destiny, both foretell and forth tell, but should point to Christ. Prophecy should be redemptive and gospel-centered in its spirit and message.

The five-fold ministry or ascension gifts of Jesus are given to the church as laid out in Ephesians 4. The purpose of these gifts is for us to represent Jesus. Prophets of the altar lift up the Lamb of God and proclaim redemption through the testimony of Jesus.

---

7. Revelation 19:10b NKJV

Chapter 10

Altars Gone Wrong

"In his book *When a Nation Forgets God,* Erwin Lutzer retells one Christian's story of living in Hitler's Germany. The man wrote:

I lived in Germany during the Nazi Holocaust. I considered myself a Christian. We heard stories of what was happening to the Jews, but we tried to distance ourselves from it, because what could anyone do to stop it?

A railroad track ran behind our small church, and each Sunday morning we could hear the whistle in the distance and then the wheels coming over the tracks. We became disturbed when we heard the cries coming from the train as it passed by. We realized that it was carrying Jews like cattle in the cars!

Week after week the whistle would blow. We dreaded to hear the sound of those wheels because we knew that we would hear the cries of the Jews en route to a death camp. Their screams tormented us.

We knew the time the train was coming, and when we heard the whistle blow we began singing hymns. By the time the train came past our church, we were singing at the top of our voices. If we heard the screams, we sang more loudly and soon we heard them no more.

Years have passed, and no one talks about it anymore. But I still hear that train whistle in my sleep. God forgive me; forgive all of us who called ourselves Christians yet did nothing to intervene."[1]

What a horrific story of the holocaust and the church literally drowning the voices of their fellow countrymen with songs of worship as they are being taken to their death. It's easy to think how cowardly and evil those actions were in history past, but we still live in a world of injustices where babies are aborted, people are trafficked for sex and labor slavery, the poor are oppressed, widows are taken advantage of and children age out of our foster care system never being adopted.

What are we doing about the things God cares about and the evil in our own day?

The altar goes wrong in one of two ways. We use the altar to cover for our sins, thinking our piety cancels out our disobedience; or we build altars to idols and don't worship God alone.

God's Rejection of Altars

Throughout most of the Scriptures, we are called to the altar. This entire book is about the power of altars, but there is actually a place where altars become a point of judgement in our lives. God is not interested in His people performing at the altar like it's some kind of theater.

That's exactly what the altar becomes, a theater, when we pretend we are faithful to God with our offerings, prayers and songs but then live in rebellion to Him. God doesn't just want Sunday worship; He wants honor with every area of our lives.

Earlier in this book, we looked at what Isaiah prophesied about this, but let's see more of that prophecy:

"The multitude of your sacrifices— what are they to me?" says the Lord. "I have more than enough burnt offerings, of rams and the fat of fattened animals; I have no pleasure in the blood of bulls and lambs and goats. When you come to appear before me, who has asked this of you, this trampling of my courts? Stop bringing meaningless offerings! Your incense is detestable to me. New Moons, Sabbaths and convocations— I cannot bear your worthless assemblies. Your New Moon feasts and your

---

1. https://www.preachingtoday.com/illustrations/2012/may/1051412.html

appointed festivals I hate with all my being. They have become a burden to me; I am weary of bearing them. When you spread out your hands in prayer, I hide my eyes from you; even when you offer many prayers, I am not listening. Your hands are full of blood! Wash and make yourselves clean. Take your evil deeds out of my sight; stop doing wrong. Learn to do right; seek justice. Defend the oppressed. Take up the cause of the fatherless; plead the case of the widow."[2]

God literally says, "I have no pleasure in your sacrifices and offerings."

It's like He's saying, "I don't want you to come to the altar anymore until you live a life of making wrong things right."

The prophets repeat this theme over and over again. We see that when God rejects His altar, the nation loses itself.

"The Lord has rejected his altar and abandoned his sanctuary. He has given the walls of her palaces into the hands of the enemy; they have raised a shout in the house of the Lord as on the day of an appointed festival."[3]

> **It does not impress God if we love our time alone with Him, but don't show love to the people we see regularly in our lives.**

When the altar was forsaken, the nation was overtaken. How true is that today, when God's people forsake the altar, other influences conquer and invade the purity of our faith.

Micah tells us what God wants and doesn't want from us. "With what shall I come before the Lord and bow down before the exalted God? Shall I come before him with burnt offerings, with calves a year old? Will the Lord be pleased with thousands of rams, with ten thou-

---

2. Isaiah 1:11-17
3. Lamentations 2:7

sand rivers of olive oil? Shall I offer my firstborn for my transgression, the fruit of my body for the sin of my soul? He has shown you, O mortal, what is good. And what does the Lord require of you? To act justly and to love mercy and to walk humbly with your God."[4]

God doesn't want us at the altar unless we are acting justly, loving mercy, and walking with God in humility.

The prophet Amos has some of the strongest words for Israel. God, who commanded offerings at the altar and festivals for His people to remember His covenant, tells them, ""I hate, I despise your religious festivals; your assemblies are a stench to me. Even though you bring me burnt offerings and grain offerings, I will not accept them. Though you bring choice fellowship offerings, I will have no regard for them. Away with the noise of your songs! I will not listen to the music of your harps. But let justice roll on like a river, righteousness like a never-failing stream!"[5]

He doesn't want them to perform.

The God who can't stay away from praise and worship no longer wanted songs. He wasn't interested in a show that left the culture devoid of justice and righteousness.

We not only see God reject offerings, prayers and worship at altars in the Old Testament, He also rejects the altar in the New Testament when we fail to walk in true repentance and obedience from the heart.

Jesus taught us in the Sermon on the Mount that we should not pursue a vertical encounter with God in worship if we don't resolve our horizontal issues with one another.

Jesus said, ""Therefore, if you are offering your gift at the altar and there remember that your brother or sister has something against you, leave your gift there in front of the altar. First go and be reconciled to them; then come and offer your gift."[6]

Jesus taught this multiple times, that our prayers will be hindered if we don't forgive people when we stand to pray.

A pastor once told me a story of being betrayed by some people he

---

4. Micah 6:6-8
5. Amos 5:21-24
6. Matthew 5:23-24

dearly loved in his church. He caught wind of what was happening, but the people who betrayed him didn't know he was aware of their actions. They acted so nice to his face but were working against his leadership behind his back.

He ended up in a place of anguish before the Lord on a mission trip. As he was praying one night, he poured out his heart to God about the hurt and pain of the whole situation. God spoke to him that all he was to do was to love them.

> **We should not pursue a vertical encounter with God in worship if we don't resolve our horizontal issues with one another.**

As he meditated on God's word to love these people, he felt this rise in his heart: "You don't have two hearts. You don't have a heart for God and a heart for people. You only have one heart. If you close your heart to people, you close your heart to God."

As I listened to his story, all of a sudden the teachings of Jesus became so real to me. If our heart is closed to others, our heart is closed to God. We can't receive the work of His Spirit. Forgiveness and reconciliation is a major key to the effectiveness of whether our prayers will be heard at altars.

This pastor's obedience caused a shift in the situation when his heart changed to love those who betrayed him.

John wrote in his first letter to the church, "Whoever claims to love God yet hates a brother or sister is a liar. For whoever does not love their brother and sister, whom they have seen, cannot love God, whom they have not seen."[7]

We have to be so careful in the prayer movement that we don't give ourselves over to being hyper spiritual. It's easy to get lifted up in pride

---

7. 1 John 4:20

while being disciplined in our prayer lives and compare ourselves to others who are struggling to pray. But it does not impress God if we love our time alone with Him, but don't show love to the people we see regularly in our lives.

It's easy to be in a prayer time and enjoy God's presence, making declarations about how we will do anything for Him, telling Him how we want Him to break our heart for what breaks His, but then leave that time of prayer and become so frustrated with the people we interact with all day.

God wants the altar to be a place of authenticity that causes our hearts to be contrite and humble, a place of transformation, so that we carry out His love and justice to a hurting and dying world.

Often conservative churches do well upholding God's love for righteousness and His hatred for immorality, while liberal churches do well upholding the causes of feeding the poor and looking after the disadvantaged.

God is looking for His people to care about both.

Altars that please the Lord, even in the New Testament, show faithfulness to God in morality and integrity as well as looking after the poor and forgotten. "Religion that God our Father accepts as pure and faultless is this: to look after orphans and widows in their distress and to keep oneself from being polluted by the world."[8]

Altars to Idols

The only way altars go wrong is not just when we use altars to God and our offerings to cover up for our rebellion and cruelty as a people, but also when we build altars to other gods.

Jeremiah prophesies the word of the Lord about this very thing, "My people have committed two sins: They have forsaken me, the spring of living water, and have dug their own cisterns, broken cisterns that cannot hold water."[9]

We humans are worshippers, if we don't worship God we not only

---

8. James 1:27
9. Jeremiah 2:13

forsake Him, we end up worshipping at some other altar. We leave the source of living water for something broken that we create and holds no water.

The first of the 10 Commandments God gave Moses is, "You shall have no other gods before me."[10] And in the next commandment, God forbids creating idols because He is a jealous God.

People misunderstand what it means for God to be jealous. Many only see jealousy as rooted in insecurity, but when we understand who God is, as the all-wise and all-powerful Creator of the universe, His jealousy is a characteristic of His sanity.

Imagine your children playing in the backyard, constructing a form out of dirt and rocks, and then telling you they will no longer listen to you, because these things they have created are their true parents. Your jealousy, in that case, would be for them to honor the truth and reality about who you are as their parents.

All throughout Israel's history, especially in the time of the Judges and Kings, Israel went through cycles of honoring the Lord and then turning their backs on Him and worshipping idols. The Kings that pleased God tore down the altars to idols and their high places of worship. God "will not share His glory with another."[11]

Faithfulness to God alone at His altar and the rejection of false gods at the altar of idols brought the blessing of God upon His people.

This pattern is not only seen in the Old Testament but in the New Testament as well. John the Beloved wrote, "Dear children, keep yourselves from idols."[12]

Idolatry was a major problem for people to overcome in the times of the New Testament Scriptures, and they are still a problem for us today. We are all worshippers as humans. We were made to worship God, but we are quick to fill that place which belongs to Him alone with other gods and other loves. They are certainly lesser gods and lesser loves, but they rob Him of the glory of who He is.

There are more and more traditional idols adorning western culture,

---

10. Exodus 20:3
11. Isaiah 42:8
12. 1 John 5:21

being used in homes and gardens as decorations, but idols can be anything we give our worship to. Our culture is full of greed, materialism, sensuality, pride and jealousy. Money, fame and power promise us that with more of them we feel secure, protected and significant. These are all things that are supposed to come from God.

The apostle Paul warned about idolatry in both of his letters to the Corinthian church. They excelled in spiritual gifts and the work of the Holy Spirit, yet God wanted them to walk in purity as well as to know His power.

Here are some of the strong words for the Christians in Corinth: "What agreement is there between the temple of God and idols? For we are the temple of the living God. As God has said: "I will live with them and walk among them, and I will be their God, and they will be my people." Therefore, "Come out from them and be separate", says the Lord. Touch no unclean thing, and I will receive you." And "I will be a Father to you, and you will be my sons and daughters, says the Lord Almighty. Therefore, since we have these promises, dear friends, let us purify ourselves from everything that contaminates body and spirit, perfecting holiness out of reverence for God.""[13]

To separate from any mixture with idols, we need the fear of the Lord. We are a temple of the Holy Spirit as His church. We have promises that God will walk with us and be our Father.

With God's presence and care secured for us through Christ, why yearn for another god? All we need is God. He has given us Himself freely and fully. Altars can have demonic and Satanic power, but the true altars release the power of God Almighty! All He wants from us is the honor and glory due His name.

May the altars of our hearts, homes, churches and regions have no mixture of worship to false gods.

---

13. 2 Corinthians 6:16-7:1

Chapter 11

Obedience over Sacrifice

What if I can make a lot of money doing something bad but I give money to a good cause? What if I buy lotto tickets and if I win, I give a double tithe? How about fifty percent? How about I give ninety percent of a billion dollar prize? Think how much good that money could do for the kingdom of God?

I remember when my children were toddlers and they would color on a wall or a piece of furniture that they knew they weren't supposed to color on. I would tell them to stop and as I moved towards them, the closer I got, the faster and harder their little hand moved to make as much of a mess as possible.

It was like they must have thought, "Well, I'm already in trouble for this. I may as well do as much as possible while I still can."

I remember almost laughing at their little rebellion because I realized I can be like that with God too. Something in our human nature likes to negotiate with compromise.

The altar is not a place for cutting deals with God.

I remember hearing a common story about men in the Greatest Generation or Baby Boomers whose wives were Christians, but they weren't. The common quip I heard from these men, "Me and the Big Guy upstairs have an understanding."

There is no such understanding where you get to negotiate with God a gospel package of your own making.

King Saul was the first king God appointed in Israel after His people cried out for one. He was making some rather poor choices as king, but none of his choices were as poor as the time he tried to use the altar to cover up his rebellion against God.

God told Saul to wipe out Amalek. He said to destroy the people, the children and all the animals. But Saul failed to do so. He left the king alive and kept all the good animals alive to keep as the spoils of war.

Then he did something so spiritual, he went and sacrificed animals to the Lord.

The prophet Samuel was called by the Lord to respond to the very king he had anointed over Israel.

"So Samuel said: "Has the Lord as great delight in burnt offerings and sacrifices, As in obeying the voice of the Lord? Behold, to obey is better than sacrifice, And to heed than the fat of rams. For rebellion is as the sin of witchcraft, And stubbornness is as iniquity and idolatry. Because you have rejected the word of the Lord, He also has rejected you from being king.""[1]

What a blow.

Saul begged to get back in God's good graces, but God told Samuel that since Saul had once again rejected Him, He was rejecting Saul as king.

And here we see it: God desires obedience over sacrifice.

Samuel says that "rebellion is as the sin of witchcraft."

Have you ever noticed that?

When you do something rebellious, it can feel really good. Rebellion has a bewitching power.

It's why we can be confused in our flesh, because doing the wrong thing can feel great and doing the right thing can feel bad.

Rebellion puts a spell on us.

There is something spiritual about taking things into your own hands and doing something for your pleasure. Whether it's the shoplifters high that thieves say they experience, or the excitement of

---

1. I Samuel 15:22-23 NKJV

sneaking where you shouldn't go to see if you won't get caught; we can all testify that rebellion can feel good for a moment even if the results are disastrous.

> **God forbid we use the altar to cover up for our rebellion and somehow think that God will receive our half-baked offering.**

God doesn't want our offerings to say sorry for our mistakes at the altar when He could have had our obedience in the first place. We must be careful not to think of ourselves as overly spiritual because of how much we pray or how passionately we worship God on a Sunday.

Over the years in ministry, there have been a few times when someone appears so spiritual and pious, but they are dishonorable in secret. We can fool others, but we never fool God.

God forbid we use the altar to cover up for our rebellion and somehow think that God will receive our half-baked offering.

After the prophet Nathan confronted King David for his sin of adultery and murder, David wrote Psalm 51. He was broken over his sin and said "For You do not desire sacrifice, or else I would give it; You do not delight in burnt offering. The sacrifices of God are a broken spirit, A broken and a contrite heart— These, O God, You will not despise."[2]

God is looking for hearts that are surrendered in obedience to Him first, and for repentant hearts that truly sorrow over their sin when they have failed to obey.

---

2. Psalms 51:16-17 NKJV

Obedience is Not a Bad Word

My dad told me two things a lot growing up.

I can almost hear him coming down the hall and saying it once again, "I know you know, but do you do?"

He would say, "Son, clean your room. Do your homework. Help your mom with this."

I would reply while trying to get him to go away, "I know, Dad."

His response, "I know you know, but do you do?"

And the other thing he would often say is, "If you love me, you will obey me."

My dad was a very loving father. He didn't say these things harshly; he said them to guide me into the truth.

Western Christians think so analytically that we have separated obedience from faith, or faith from works.

A lot of Christians have been sold the idea that in the Old Testament you got saved through your works, but in the New Testament you get saved by faith. So, we have reduced faith to believing the right list of doctrines about God.

But the writer of Hebrews shows us we are all saved by faith, who look to Jesus. The Old Testament people were saved by faith looking forward to the cross and us New Testament people are saved by faith in looking back to the cross. But our faith is not only in happy thoughts about God. Biblically, faith is a place of trust that is demonstrated by our obedience born out of love.

Jesus said that all the 613 laws and commandments and the core message of the prophets can be summed up in two commands. "Jesus replied: " 'Love the Lord your God with all your heart and with all your soul and with all your mind.' This is the first and greatest commandment. And the second is like it: 'Love your neighbor as yourself.' All the Law and the Prophets hang on these two commandments.'"[3]

Jesus quotes Deuteronomy, a book of the Law, and summarizes it all for us brilliantly. But He doesn't do away with the call to obedience.

John wrote about this in his gospel and in his first letter to the

---

3. Matthew 22:37-40

church, "And this is his command: to believe in the name of his Son, Jesus Christ, and to love one another as he commanded us."[4]

We still have commandments we are to obey as Christians. The first one is to believe in Jesus.

Our faith starts with belief in response to the love of God for us. But even our faith is obedience to a commandment. From that place of loving God, we are to also love others. This is not a burden for us. The call to obedience is a call to Christlikeness.

My dad really got one of his famous lines from Jesus, ""If you love me, keep my commands."[5]

It's simple. Love manifests through our obedience.

I've heard enough Christians say that God loves you no matter what, even when you disobey. That is true, but it's incomplete because it gives the impression that disobedience is okay with God.

Healthy Relationships don't exist without obedience out of love. We are deceived if we think we can persist in disobedience while also thinking we are loving our Savior.

I'm afraid for all the Christians being misled by preachers who say that obedience is a dead work. If we try to do things to earn God's love, we will fail miserably. "This is love: not that we loved God, but that he loved us and sent his Son as an atoning sacrifice for our sins. We love because he first loved us."[6]

So we can't love God in our own strength. It takes God to love God. It takes God's love in us first, to empower us to love God and love others. But our love for God is still a required response for the Christian life.

We are called to obedience in the great commission, "Therefore go and make disciples of all nations, baptizing them in the name of the Father and of the Son and of the Holy Spirit, and teaching them to obey everything I have commanded you. And surely I am with you always, to the very end of the age.""[7]

---

4. 1 John 3:23
5. John 14:15
6. 1 John 4:10,19
7. Matthew 28:19-20

We are called to obey in the greatest commandments listed above. We are even called to not only believe in the gospel, but to obey it, "But they have not all obeyed the gospel..."[8]

"He will punish those who do not know God and do not obey the gospel of our Lord Jesus."[9]

Obedience is not just a theme of the Old Testament it is a major part of the New Testament life and the way of following Jesus.

I want to assure you I don't believe that my obedience or my works save me, but I want you to see that we shouldn't separate our faith from obedience. We are saved only by grace through faith. Jesus saves us, plain and simple.

But a saved life produces the good fruit of obedience. "For by grace you have been saved through faith, and that not of yourselves; it is the gift of God, not of works, lest anyone should boast. For we are His workmanship, created in Christ Jesus for good works, which God prepared beforehand that we should walk in them."[10]

God's grace saves us through faith, and then we do works which Christ Jesus has already prepared for us.

The fathers of the Christian faith would not have recognized any disparity between being saved by grace and living a holy life of obedience. The goal of the Christian life is conformity to Christ's image. This is what the Eastern church refers to as Theosis, and similarly, what the Western church refers to as sanctification.

"See what great love the Father has lavished on us, that we should be called children of God! And that is what we are! The reason the world does not know us is that it did not know him. Dear friends, now we are children of God, and what we will be has not yet been made known. But we know that when Christ appears, we shall be like him, for we shall see him as he is. All who have this hope in him purify themselves, just as he is pure."[11]

---

8. Romans 10:16 NKJV
9. 2 Thessalonians 1:8
10. Ephesians 2:8-10
11. 1 John 3:1-3 NIV

This incredible love calls us to be prepared for the day we meet Him and become like Him.

A hallmark of the last days will be lawlessness and wickedness.

Jesus said, "Because of the increase of wickedness, the love of most will grow cold, but the one who stands firm to the end will be saved."[12]

We often hear about how being religious or focused on works can cause us to lose our first love, which is certainly warned about in Galatians. But Jesus said that disobedience or wickedness (lawlessness in the NKJV) actually causes the love of many to grow cold.

We can be so confident in God's love, but when we let compromise in and give way to lawlessness, we are warned of not having the endurance to be saved.

Obedience is an opportunity to show God our love by putting His desires first, and to spurn the witchcraft of rebellion. Just like my dad's other lesson, God doesn't want us just to know the right things, He wants us to do the right things.

"Thus also faith by itself, if it does not have works, is dead."[13]

The altar is not a place for sacrifice to try and hide our disobedience.

Sometimes sacrifice is obedience. As in, sometimes sacrificing our future, our dreams, our wants and desires on the altar is obedience.

Other times, a sacrifice is a half-hearted attempt to hope God overlooks our rebellion.

Give God a life of obedience out of love for the One who loves you beyond measure.

---

12. Matthew 24:12-13
13. James 2:17 NKJV

Chapter 12

Priests at Altars or Sages on Stages

We have been in a remodeling project in our church for many years. We've made a church out of a warehouse. Ever since we bought the whole building, we've raised money by faith to build out one part at a time.

One of the final spaces for us to finish is our worship center or sanctuary. As of this writing, we have almost finished this phase of our building, and we are already using it for our worship services and prayer meetings.

It's actually become a beautiful space, especially for a warehouse.

One of the things that's happened as we have remodeled our building is deciding what to call different rooms or spaces.

Do we use words like foyer or lobby?

Do we say fellowship hall or the commons?

Do we say sanctuary or auditorium?

One of our members at the time brought up that we shouldn't call the elevated place at the front a stage. He said for performance we call it a stage, but we should call it a platform.

A platform is about a space that elevates a message.

I thought it was a good point, but I think even better than a platform, we ought to call it an altar.

The altar shouldn't be seen as only the place at the edge of the platform where people come to kneel, pray, or worship. The whole platform should be considered an altar.

For every song and every singer, every note played by every musician, every sermon preached by every preacher and every action should be presented on the altar as a sacrifice of praise.

Why should someone coming up to seek God at the front of the sanctuary be considered coming to the altar, but where I stand as a preacher it's somehow different?

Why should the sinner begging for mercy come to an altar call, but I, the preacher, do not realize I need the same mercy at the same altar?

I never read John Piper's book *Brothers, we are not Professionals*, but I feel like the title almost says it all. American churchianity has become filled with entertainment and performance.

Jesus constantly used the word hypocrites to describe and rebuke the religious leaders of His day. We often conceive nowadays of the spiritual connotation of this word, meaning someone who is two-faced or living a double life.

Well, in Jesus' day it was a word to describe an actor who went on a stage and played a part. Too often, I am afraid the church has fallen into the same trap. We aren't just hypocrites because we fail to live up to our message; we are designing services as professionals to entertain people, while failing to impress God.

My dad told me a story that a group of Chinese church leaders were taken on a tour of some of America's largest and most "successful" churches. After the tour was over, when the leaders from China were asked what they thought about the American church, their response was chilling, "It's amazing what the American church has built without the Holy Spirit."

Purify the Fire

If it's true that the culture is downstream of her cults or that the church is the conscience of a nation, then how crooked is a nation whose churches are full of compromise? If the nation goes the way of the church, the church goes the way of the pulpit.

As we looked at earlier in this book, the jobs of the priests in the tabernacle included making sure the fire never went out on the altar and to burn incense before the Lord.

A priest's first job is ministry unto the Lord. In Leviticus, Aaron the High Priest's sons become casual and disrespectful with the fire they are supposed to steward. "Then Nadab and Abihu, the sons of Aaron, each took his censer and put fire in it, put incense on it, and offered profane fire before the Lord, which He had not commanded them. So fire went out from the Lord and devoured them, and they died before the Lord. And Moses said to Aaron, "This is what the Lord spoke, saying: 'By those who come near Me I must be regarded as holy; And before all the people I must be glorified.' " So Aaron held his peace."[1]

So, just like that, Aaron's sons took the holy fire and offered it to the Lord in their own way. They literally proved the old proverb, "If you play with fire, you're going to get burned."

They brought a profane fire before the Lord and the Lord consumed them with His fire. God wants to be approached with reverence and honor. If the priest compromised the fire, it affects the rest of the people of God.

If pastors compromise their ministry, the whole church suffers.

If pastors compromise their ministry, the whole church suffers. This is why God holds leaders accountable at a higher level. Their actions affect the whole of the people they lead.

We get so concerned about what the pagans are doing in the world. But God says judgement starts in the church. "For it is time for judg-

---

1. Leviticus 10:1-3 NKJV

ment to begin with God's household; and if it begins with us, what will the outcome be for those who do not obey the gospel of God?"[2]

If the church is judged more strictly than the world, who in the church is judged first?

"Not many of you should become teachers, my fellow believers, because you know that we who teach will be judged more strictly."[3]

The judgement that begins in God's house begins with the leadership. It's the preachers behind pulpits and the teachers of God's Word who must walk in a greater accountability to live a life that honors God.

It's easy to impress people from a platform or a stage, but it's time to lay on the altar.

Our charisma and gifting will make us known on earth, but it's our faithfulness to Jesus in character and obedience that will make us known in heaven. If the pure fire of the Holy Spirit is to be kept burning in the church, that pure fire needs to burn in the lives of us pastors.

Shooting our Wounded?

In 2020, I was trying to discern the times we were living in culturally, politically and in the church. As I prayed with a heavy heart in that season, I felt the Lord speak to me and say we were entering a time in the culture and the church that would be known as "the great unveiling."

I began to see in the prophets Jeremiah and Ezekiel that God exposed false prophets, false pastors and the emptiness of idolatry.

It's been appalling and shocking to me to see the amount of leadership failure in the Pentecostal and charismatic church world these past several years. Adultery, sexual abuse, spiritual abuse, deceptive prophetic tactics and manipulation have been exposed at a level I've never witnessed in my life.

To some degree, I'm not surprised that people or leaders sin, but worse than the sin is the cover-ups and weak theology to make excuses for these behaviors. As these exposures of sin have taken place, many

---

2. 1 Peter 4:17
3. James 3:1 NIV

Christians run to the defense of fallen ministers, decrying those calling for accountability as judgmental and tools of Satan.

I hear over and over again, even after a pastor has groomed someone, taken them into a secret ongoing sexual relationship and spiritually manipulated them, that when the pastor gets exposed publicly, and is disciplined, people say something like, "The church is the only army that shoots our own wounded."

In the case of a pastor preying on a young woman in his ministry and using her for his own selfish needs, how is he looked at as the wounded?

I realize the sayings that "hurt people, hurt people" and "wounded people, wound people." But in the case of a leader abusing someone in his or her church, the leader is the wound-er not the wounded.

Popular ministries are teaching that if a leader fails in their position, we should just keep it secret because it's not anyone's business to know about people's private lives.

But isn't this just really a play to make sure that the show keeps going on? I mean, if the church is built on a stage, then by all means keep the people, money and opportunities flowing.

But if the church is built on the altar, then we bring our sins and failings before the Lord and even before others to deal with the heart of what's happening.

If we are espousing truth from a pulpit and violating that same truth, isn't this the very thing that Jesus showed up to condemn?

Many leaders in hidden sin are appealing to vague principles from Scriptures about Noah, David, or the Matthew 18 principle when they sin. Noah's nakedness being uncovered by his son Ham while he was drunk in Genesis 9 has been used by ministries to say we shouldn't expose a leader's sin because Ham was cursed for doing so. But Bible scholars demonstrate that in Noah's day, and in ancient near east cultures, exposing someone's nakedness was not about undressing them, it was about taking advantage of their drunken state and usually having a sexual relationship with the drunk person's spouse while they were out of it.[4]

---

4. Noah's Nakedness and the Curse on Canaan (Genesis 9:20-27) by John Sietze

While it may be difficult to ascertain exactly what happened from the vague language, it's evident this story is not about covering up for church leaders when they sin.

David sinned with Bathsheba, and later in the New Testament, as Paul is preaching in Acts 13, Paul says that David was a man after God's heart. This is very hopeful for anyone who has struggled with sin to know they can be restored and honored because of the grace of God.

But we have to remember that this sin also cost David greatly and God did not turn a blind eye to it. God restores fallen sinners and even fallen leaders. But David's moral failing, judgement and restoration is not a standard for leadership in the body of Christ.

Whatever great things we build with our anointing, we can cause to be destroyed with our character.

So often, people will appeal to Matthew 18 as the way to handle these situations when leaders sin morally.

But Matthew 18 is about confronting someone who sins against you as a brother or sister in the Lord. There are escalating actions to take if someone doesn't respond to you privately. Matthew 18 is very important for relational restoration where sin has occurred, but not in a leadership scenario.

If a leader sexually abuses someone in their own office, according to Matthew 18, the abuse victim is supposed to go privately back to the office of the abuser and ask them to please repent?

This is not right or healthy.

Bergsma and Scott Walker Hahn https://scholarlypublishingcollective.org/sblpress/jbl/article-abstract/124/1/25/179379/Noah-s-Nakedness-and-the-Curse-on-Canaan-Genesis-9?redirectedFrom=fulltext

If these leadership failures arise to the level of a crime, they need to be reported to the police.

So what is the way?

The pattern for leadership standards and how to deal with their failure is clearly laid out by Paul in his first letter to Timothy. "Do not entertain an accusation against an elder unless it is brought by two or three witnesses. But those elders who are sinning you are to reprove before everyone, so that the others may take warning. I charge you, in the sight of God and Christ Jesus and the elect angels, to keep these instructions without partiality, and to do nothing out of favoritism."[5]

Why are we preferring Old Testament stories and Matthew 18 over the clear instruction we are given for New Testament church leadership?

When you have a public ministry, you have public privileges and responsibilities. When leaders sin, especially those who make good money from conferences and book sales, they have benefited greatly from a public ministry.

I don't have a problem with a minister being fairly compensated and being a successful author.

But the principle of Scripture is that the more you benefit from something, the more accountable you have to be.

So, if you are preaching or writing to thousands or millions of people, then you are accountable to God first, but then the people you serve in the gospel.

Whatever great things we build with our anointing, we can cause to be destroyed with our character.

I love pastors and ministers of the gospel. I believe in God's grace for leaders. All of us leaders and pastors fall short in some areas and sin. No leaders are going to live sinlessly and flawlessly. Pastors deal with a lot of judgements, gossip and hurtful behavior by the people they lay down their lives for.

I'm not siding with people who are tearing down leaders and trying to bring down ministries. But if we can't say that sexual sin, spiritual abuse, lying about getting prophetic words and other manipulative practices is disqualifying, we aren't fooling anyone. This is not a good

---

5. 1 Timothy 5:19-21

look for us, and we are losing the next generation with our cover-up attempts that don't produce good fruit.

Reading the prophets and the New Testament Scriptures about God's standards and judgment of leaders, it's apparent to me that the exposure of sin in today's church leadership is not primarily the work of Satan but the work of God Himself. God said through the prophet Ezekiel, "" 'Therefore, you shepherds, hear the word of the Lord: As surely as I live, declares the Sovereign Lord, because my flock lacks a shepherd and so has been plundered and has become food for all the wild animals, and because my shepherds did not search for my flock but cared for themselves rather than for my flock, therefore, you shepherds, hear the word of the Lord: This is what the Sovereign Lord says: I am against the shepherds and will hold them accountable for my flock. I will remove them from tending the flock so that the shepherds can no longer feed themselves. I will rescue my flock from their mouths, and it will no longer be food for them."[6]

God does not tolerate the mistreatment of his flock.

Standards

We need to simply return to the clear instruction of Scripture and walk in the fear of the Lord.

We need a restoration of standards for leadership.

There are the obvious ones, like Paul's list of qualifications for elders and deacons. The other standards, though, are mixed up with what has become a normal part of church in America.

We expect pastors to be marriage and family experts, politically informed, possess real estate and contract knowledge, manage teams, preach life-changing sermons every week, provide counseling, attend family events and more.

The demands of ministry can break your soul.

The late leadership expert, Peter Drucker, said that according to his research, the four toughest jobs in America are President of the United

---

6. Ezekiel 34:7-10

States, a hospital administrator, a university president, and the pastor of a local church.[7]

With all the complexity in the ministry these days, we need to return as pastors to the simplicity of the call of Jesus. The call is not to first preach or teach, it's a call to be with Jesus.

I remember Graham Cooke shared while teaching once, that "The secret to the anointing is to spend most of it on Jesus."

Mary of Bethany was not a pastor when she anointed Jesus with her costly perfume, but she shows us the way of the altar, a life laid down for the glory of Jesus.

The minimum standard for ministers is about putting Jesus first in our own lives, not ministering *for* Him first, but *to* Him first.

We need to embrace the spiritual disciplines that allow our soul to be nurtured in God's love and presence. Our prayer life, solitude and time in Scripture are necessary as the foundation of a healthy ministry. We need to become fascinated with God and become a person of one thing.

May God restore the pastorate and ministry leadership of His house to a single focus, "One thing I ask from the Lord, this only do I seek: that I may dwell in the house of the Lord all the days of my life, to gaze on the beauty of the Lord and to seek him in his temple."[8]

The Altar is Our Hope

The altar is our hope for the restoration of purity and power to the ministry of the church. God is sick of our PR games and NDAs. The church has become a business in so many ways, as long as we fill the seats, fill the offering baskets and have all the signs of outward success, it's like the show must go on. We aren't fooling God and, quite frankly, less and less people seem to be fooled as well.

I have not lost heart though because of the goodness of God and the power of His promises.

I was blessed to live in a home with a dad who handled leadership

---

7. https://baptistcourier.com/2015/02/letter-toughest-job-america/
8. Psalms 27:4

failure with both grace and integrity. My dad made a place for public rebuke, public repentance and restoration. I've seen him have people confess their sins as pastors, deacons and elders to church members and watch our community respond in forgiveness while consequences still occurred. I watched him have to make gut wrenching decisions and cooperate with authorities.

I've heard that some of the people who were disciplined in love publicly believe their marriage was saved as a result of the discipline. We don't have to be vengeful or mean spirited in discipline on the one hand, nor do we need to overlook offenses and ignore Biblical instruction on the other. We need to walk these things out in grace and truth.

At the altar we can grieve, repent, forgive, heal and encounter the restorative power of God.

How about we spend time in prayer and deep repentance for the failures in leadership?

How about we do as Jesus says and go seek the restoration of relationship before presenting our gifts at the altar?

> **If we would get back to doing God's ministry, God's way, I believe we would have such an outpouring of God's power in our churches across this land.**

How about we protect the purity of the ministry with public rebuke, like Paul instructed Timothy?

If we would get back to doing God's ministry, God's way, I believe we would have such an outpouring of God's power in our churches across this land.

We need to get back to the altar and lay down our lives, our sins, our callings, our failures and let God decide what gets to be raised back up. Maybe some of our ministries should die, and others He will raise to new life.

Am I saying there is no way back for fallen ministers?

No.

But the way back for restoration is not hiding, minimizing and compromising our way back to platforms. The way back for restoration is a true return to the altar of deep and authentic repentance.

I wonder what would happen if fallen ministers really took to heart the Scriptures above the voice of consultants and got low enough at the altar.

There will be no holy fire in our churches if the leaders and ministers resist being purified by the same flame they proclaim. Brothers and sisters in ministry, let us lead the way to the altar. Let us not trust in the methods and wisdom of men, let us be yielded and consecrated to our awesome God!

Chapter 13

The Glorious Invitation to Revival

In Joel, God judged His people Israel with a great army of locusts that destroyed much of the land. Then He brought a drought that wiped out even more. The land was totally destitute. The people had rebelled against God and were suffering greatly from His judgements.

The drinkers mourned, for there was no wine and no vines. The farmers mourned, for there was no grain. The priests mourned, for they had nothing to sacrifice to the Lord. Even the cattle, herds and flocks mourned because all their food was gone.

Everyone was desperate, in despair and hopeless!

So, what do you do when all hope is gone? What do you do when you've been trapped in the judgement of your own sins? What do you do when everything is lost?

Here is God's remedy:

*"Put on sackcloth, you priests, and mourn; wail, **you who minister before the altar**. Come, spend the night in sackcloth, you who minister before my God; for the grain offerings and drink offerings are withheld from the house of your God. Declare a holy fast; call a sacred assembly.*

Summon the elders and all who live in the land to the house of the Lord your God, and cry out to the Lord."[1]

""Even now," declares the Lord, "return to me with all your heart, with fasting and weeping and mourning." Rend your heart and not your garments. Return to the Lord your God, for he is gracious and compassionate, slow to anger and abounding in love, and he relents from sending calamity. Who knows? He may turn and relent and leave behind a blessing— grain offerings and drink offerings for the Lord your God. Blow the trumpet in Zion, declare a holy fast, call a sacred assembly. Gather the people, consecrate the assembly; bring together the elders, gather the children, those nursing at the breast. Let the bridegroom leave his room and the bride her chamber. **Let the priests, who minister before the Lord, weep between the portico and the altar.** *Let them say, "Spare your people, Lord. Do not make your inheritance an object of scorn, a byword among the nations. Why should they say among the peoples, 'Where is their God?' ""*[2]

God calls all the people to return to Him in fasting, weeping, and mourning in repentance. He calls everyone from every generation to consecrate an assembly and not tear their garments but their hearts.

He wants the hearts of His people.

He doesn't want a show. He wants something real from the heart.

But He especially calls to the priests and those who minister before the Lord at the altar. The priests and ministers are to weep between the portico and the altar.

There is nothing left to offer the Lord in the land, but what He wants is His leaders and His people to give Him themselves.

What is God's response to all of this?

"Then the Lord was jealous for his land and took pity on his people. *The Lord replied to them:* **"I am sending you grain, new wine**

---

1. Joel 1:13-14
2. Joel 2:12-17

and olive oil, enough to satisfy you fully; never again will I make you an object of scorn to the nations. "I will drive the northern horde far from you, pushing it into a parched and barren land; its eastern ranks will drown in the Dead Sea and its western ranks in the Mediterranean Sea. And its stench will go up; its smell will rise." **Surely he has done great things! Do not be afraid, land of Judah; be glad and rejoice. Surely the Lord has done great things!** *Do not be afraid, you wild animals, for the pastures in the wilderness are becoming green. The trees are bearing their fruit; the fig tree and the vine yield their riches. Be glad, people of Zion, rejoice in the Lord your God, for he has given you the autumn rains because he is faithful.* **He sends you abundant showers, both autumn and spring rains, as before. The threshing floors will be filled with grain; the vats will overflow with new wine and oil. "I will repay you for the years the locusts have eaten— the great locust and the young locust, the other locusts and the locust swarm**— *my great army that I sent among you.* **You will have plenty to eat, until you are full, and you will praise the name of the Lord your God, who has worked wonders for you; never again will my people be shamed. Then you will know that I am in Israel, that I am the Lord your God, and that there is no other; never again will my people be shamed. "And afterward, I will pour out my Spirit on all people. Your sons and daughters will prophesy, your old men will dream dreams, your young men will see visions. Even on my servants, both men and women, I will pour out my Spirit in those days. I will show wonders in the heavens and on the earth, blood and fire and billows of smoke. The sun will be turned to darkness and the moon to blood before the coming of the great and dreadful day of the Lord. And everyone who calls on the name of the Lord will be saved;** *for on Mount Zion and in Jerusalem there will be deliverance, as the Lord has said, even among the survivors whom the Lord calls.*"[3]

---

3. Joel 2:18-32 NIV

God's response was to restore everything.

Heaven's response to our return to the Lord and repentance releases revival.

When the priests and people return in humility and wholehearted surrender to the Lord, the Lord sends the rain, everything flourishes, and God restores everything that was destroyed. Ultimately, God will pour out His Spirit and it will be known that God is in the midst of His people once again.

God's judgment results in the withdrawal of His presence.

The reward of revival is Him, the presence of His presence.

What's the Invitation?

In one of the best teaching series I've ever heard on revival, Pastor Mark Brattrud gave us this definition of revival, "Revival is God's response to our response to His revelation."

God has revealed to us His righteous remedy for our rebellion and ruin. When we respond to His glorious invitation, He responds with revival.

Many believe that prayer, fasting and repentance are unnecessary because of the new covenant. We have a union with God in Christ because of the gospel. We are reconciled by faith, no doubt. God's grace is so massive for our brokenness.

But what has happened to the fruit of abiding?

If I am in union with Christ, and my heart, my home, my church and my region are manifesting sinfulness and brokenness, is there not more for me and my people in that union? If we are in Christ, where are the fruits of repentance and fruits of the Spirit?

Even in New Covenant reality, where Christ Jesus has spread Himself upon the altar and we can only offer our lives to Him because of the grace He provides, we are still called to the place of the altar.

Jesus Himself revealed to the apostle of love, John the Beloved, that He was examining the seven churches of Asia Minor. The church in Laodicea,

> *"To the angel of the church in Laodicea write: These are the words of the*

Amen, the faithful and true witness, the ruler of God's creation. **I know your deeds, that you are neither cold nor hot. I wish you were either one or the other! So, because you are lukewarm—neither hot nor cold—I am about to spit you out of my mouth.** *You say, 'I am rich; I have acquired wealth and do not need a thing.' But* **you do not realize that you are wretched, pitiful, poor, blind and naked. I counsel you to buy from me gold refined in the fire, so you can become rich; and white clothes to wear, so you can cover your shameful nakedness; and salve to put on your eyes, so you can see. Those whom I love I rebuke and discipline. So be earnest and repent.** *Here I am!* **I stand at the door and knock. If anyone hears my voice and opens the door, I will come in and eat with that person, and they with me. To the one who is victorious, I will give the right to sit with me on my throne, just as I was victorious and sat down with my Father on his throne. Whoever has ears, let them hear what the Spirit says to the churches.**"[4]

These seven churches had various levels of success and failure in God's eyes.

And the church in Laodicea gets a huge rebuke. They are lukewarm and Jesus is warning of His judgment against them if they don't repent.

He rebukes us out of love, but He also invites us into victory over our halfhearted, lukewarm compromise. He is knocking at our door and pursuing fellowship with us in our rebellion.

The problem with Laodicea is they thought they were doing great, but they were totally deceived. We don't know our own heart without letting the light of Jesus shine in us and examine us.

The power of the invitation is that those who truly come before the Lord at the altar of repentance and authentically let God deal with the issues of their heart and character are rewarded with a seat on God's throne. Those who live at the altar get to join the One on the throne. Jesus shares His victory with us. He humbled Himself and He is exalted.

---

4. Revelation 3:14-22

God promises us the same thing. "Humble yourselves, therefore, under God's mighty hand, that he may lift you up in due time."[5]

Brother Paul Cornish used to tell us that "The revival of iniquity and righteousness are always running in parallel. When times are getting dark and evil, don't lose heart, God is about to raise up a remedy of revival."

The invitation is that when everything is broken, dark and dead, God will revive it all if we seek Him in prayer. "If my people, who are called by my name, will humble themselves and pray and seek my face and turn from their wicked ways, then I will hear from heaven, and I will forgive their sin and will heal their land."[6]

Ask, Seek and Knock

In Luke's account of what is famously called *The Lord's Prayer* by Protestants and the *Our Father* by Catholics, Luke expands on Jesus' teaching about prayer.

It is a powerful prayer. "He said to them, "When you pray, say: " 'Father, hallowed be your name, your kingdom come. Give us each day our daily bread. Forgive us our sins, for we also forgive everyone who sins against us. And lead us not into temptation.' """[7]

Many are more familiar with Matthew's version which expands the prayer a little bit but is overall the same.

But I want to draw attention to what is often missed here in Jesus' teaching in prayer.

After He gives us the words to pray, He tells a story about a man who gets what he wants from his friend by asking with "shameless audacity."[8]

Then Jesus says, "So I say to you: Ask and it will be given to you; seek and you will find; knock and the door will be opened to you. For

---

5. 1 Peter 5:6
6. 2 Chronicles 7:14
7. Luke 11:2-4
8. Luke 11:8

everyone who asks receives; the one who seeks finds; and to the one who knocks, the door will be opened."[9]

I've heard a lot of teaching on the Lord's prayer, and I've even heard a lot of teaching on asking, seeking and knocking, but I don't usually hear them taught together. One of the few times the disciples asked Jesus how to do something, it was to learn the secret of His prayer life. He not only tells them what to pray, but how to pray it.

Pray with shameless audacity. Pray with fervency in asking, seeking, and knocking. These are continuous, ongoing actions that result in the promises fulfilled of receiving, finding, and doors opening.

Leonard Ravenhill said, "The only reason we don't have revival is because we are willing to live without it!"[10]

Where are those asking, seeking, and knocking?

Where are the all-night prayer meetings?

Where are those who will skip meals for fasting and fully abandon themselves in surrender to God in prayer?

If the promises of God are released in and through those who practice fervent asking, seeking, and knocking prayer, why aren't we praying?

We have methods and machines in ministry, but God is looking for modern martyrs and monks who are dead to this world on the altar but alive to God in fervent prayer.

The Power of Promises

Prayer unlocks the promises. Prayer is the currency of heaven.

Prayer causes what is in the Word to become written on our hearts.

Prayer activates our faith.

Prayer is the place of repentance and unloading our griefs.

Prayer is our place of empowerment from on High.

Prayer is asking!

There is no breakthrough at the altars without asking God. And

---

9. Luke 11:9-10
10. https://quotefancy.com/quote/852417/Leonard-Ravenhill-The-only-reason-we-don-t-have-revival-is-because-we-are-willing-to-live

there is no power to pray but by abiding according to the promises of God.

Jesus said, "If you remain in me and my words remain in you, ask whatever you wish, and it will be done for you. This is to my Father's glory, that you bear much fruit, showing yourselves to be my disciples."[11]

Jesus repeated this type of promise several times in John 14-16. Jesus wants us to glorify the Father by asking Him for things we will receive in prayer. Our prayers being answered are part of the recipe of the Father's delight and joy.

> **Prayer that comes from the heart in obedience and alignment with God has the power to change the course of history and bring revival.**

Our answered prayers become the fruit of our abiding.

One of the great authors on prayer, Andrew Murray said, on this power and promise of asking, "On a thoughtful comparison of what we mostly find in books or sermons on prayer, and the teaching of the Master, we shall find one great difference: the importance assigned to the answer to prayer is by no means the same. In the former we find a great deal on the blessing of prayer as a spiritual exercise even if there be no answer, and on the reasons why we should be content without it. God's fellowship ought to be more to us than the gift we ask; God's wisdom only knows what is best; God may bestow something better than what He withholds. Though this teaching looks very high and spiritual, it is remarkable that we find nothing of it with our Lord. The more carefully we gather together all He spoke on prayer, the clearer it becomes that He wished us to think of prayer simply as the means to an

---

11. John 15:7-8

end, and that the answer was to be the proof that we and our prayer are acceptable to the Father in heaven. It is not that Christ would have us count the gifts of higher value than the fellowship and favour of the Father. By no means. But the Father means the answer to be the token of His favour and of the reality of our fellowship with Him... A life marked by daily answer to prayer is the proof of our spiritual maturity; that we have indeed attained to the true abiding in Christ; that our will is truly at one with God's will; that our faith has grown strong to see and take what God has prepared for us; that the Name of Christ and His nature have taken full possession of us; and that we have been found fit to take a place among those whom God admits to His counsels, and according to whose prayer He rules the world. These are they in whom something of man's original dignity hath been restored, in whom, as they abide in Christ, His power as the all-prevailing Intercessor can manifest itself, in whom the glory of His Name is shown forth. Prayer is very blessed; the answer is more blessed still, as the response from the Father that our prayer, our faith, our will are indeed as He would wish them to be. I make these remarks with the one desire of leading my readers themselves to put together all that Christ has said on prayer, and to yield themselves to the full impression of the truth that when prayer is what it should be, or rather when we are what we should be, abiding in Christ, the answer must be expected. It will bring us out from those refuges where we have comforted ourselves with unanswered prayer. It will discover to us the place of power to which Christ has appointed His Church, and which it so little occupies. It will reveal the terrible feebleness of our spiritual life as the cause of our not knowing to pray boldly in Christ's Name. It will urge us mightily to rise to a life in the full union with Christ, and in the fulness of the Spirit, as the secret of effectual prayer. And it will so lead us on to realize our destiny: At that day: Verily, verily, I say unto you, If you shall ask anything of the Father, He will give it you in my Name: ask, and you shall receive, that your joy may be fulfilled.' Prayer that is really, spiritually, in union with Jesus, is always answered." [12]

God has given us many promises on the power of fervent, persistent,

---

12. Andrew Murray on prayer from "With Christ in the school of Prayer," Chapter 21

and heartfelt prayer. Prayer that comes from the heart in obedience and alignment with God has the power to change the course of history and bring revival. Nothing else can.

The early church father John Chrysostom said, "Prayer is an all-efficient panoply, a treasure undiminished, a mine never exhausted, a sky unobstructed by clouds, a haven unruffled by storm. It is the root, the fountain, and the mother of a thousand blessings. It exceeds a monarch's power.... I speak not of the prayer which is cold and feeble and devoid of zeal. I speak of that which proceeds from a mind outstretched, the child of a contrite spirit, the offspring of a soul converted—this is the prayer which mounts to heaven.... The power of prayer has subdued the strength of fire, bridled the rage of lions, silenced anarchy, extinguished wars, appeased the elements, expelled demons, burst the chains of death, enlarged the gates of heaven, relieved diseases, averted frauds, rescued cities from destruction, stayed the sun in its course, and arrested the progress of the thunderbolt. In sum, prayer has power to destroy whatever is at enmity with the good. I speak not of the prayer of the lips, but of the prayer that ascends from the inmost recesses of the heart."[13]

FIRE FALLS ON SACRIFICE

When King Solomon was dedicating the temple that his father David had dreamed to build for God years before, he came before the Lord with a prayer and this is what happened: "When Solomon finished praying, fire came down from heaven and consumed the burnt offering and the sacrifices, and the glory of the Lord filled the temple. The priests could not enter the temple of the Lord because the glory of the Lord filled it. When all the Israelites saw the fire coming down and the glory of the Lord above the temple, they knelt on the pavement with their faces to the ground, and they worshiped and gave thanks to the Lord, saying, "He is good; his love endures forever.""[14]

---

13. On the Incomprehensible Nature of God, Homily 5.44, 46, 57, 58.
14. 2 Chronicles 7:1-3

As Solomon and the priests laid the offerings and sacrifices on the altar, God sent the fire from heaven.

Many preachers have said, "Fire always falls on sacrifice."

It's true.

The altar is the place to give God what He wants, and His fire, His presence and His glory is our reward.

The altar is not the place we go to get what we want.

It's the place we give God what He wants, but then we get so much more.

I implore you to give God what He wants, to give your life to the altar, to be a living sacrifice.

Heaven is waiting to respond to our response to God's revelation. The revival of the altar in prayer, repentance and obedience will release the sovereign power of God to heal and change our world once again. Christian, put your faith in the altar once more. Give your life to prayer and fidelity to God. Make Christlikeness your highest pursuit. Clothe yourself in humility and fill your world with prayers. Take up your cross, take up your altar. Walk in the footsteps of Your Lord and overcome by the power of His sacrifice. History is waiting to be made by those who move heaven's heart at earth's altars.

Appendix

John Wesley's 22 Questions

These are 22 questions the members of John Wesley's Holy Club asked themselves every day in their private devotions over 200 years ago.

1. Am I consciously or unconsciously creating the impression that I am better than I really am? In other words, am I a hypocrite?
2. Am I honest in all my acts and words, or do I exaggerate?
3. Do I confidentially pass on to another what was told to me in confidence?
4. Can I be trusted?
5. Am I a slave to dress, friends, work, or habits?
6. Am I self-conscious, self-pitying, or self-justifying?
7. Did the Bible live in me today?
8. Do I give it time to speak to me everyday?
9. Am I enjoying prayer?
10. When did I last speak to someone else about my faith?
11. Do I pray about the money I spend?
12. Do I get to bed on time and get up on time?

13. Do I disobey God in anything?
14. Do I insist upon doing something about which my conscience is uneasy?
15. Am I defeated in any part of my life?
16. Am I jealous, impure, critical, irritable, touchy, or distrustful?
17. How do I spend my spare time?
18. Am I proud?
19. Do I thank God that I am not as other people, especially as the Pharisees who despised the publican?
20. Is there anyone whom I fear, dislike, disown, criticize, hold a resentment toward or disregard? If so, what am I doing about it?
21. Do I grumble or complain constantly?
22. Is Christ real to me?

Also by John Hammer

eXXXit

The Presence Series:

- The Lord of the Presence
- The Power of the Presence
- The Pursuit of the Presence
- The Wonder of the Presence

Contact

To continue to get more writing and updates from John or invite John to speak go subscribe to his Substack at johnandhammer.substack.com

About the Author

John Hammer is married to the love of his life Grace Elaine, and is a dad to four amazing children: Hailey, Emma, Justus and Addison. John is a graduate of Seattle Bible College. He loves communication through preaching, teaching, writing poetry and prose, as well as theological or philosophical conversations. He enjoys laughter at family dinners and staying active with them through Brazilian-Jiu Jitsu, Pickleball, and river walks. He and Grace are the Lead Pastors at Sonrise Christian Center in Everett, WA. He is also a co-founder of The Way and Represent Conferences. Johnandhammer.substack.com | isonrise.org

www.ingramcontent.com/pod-product-compliance
Lightning Source LLC
Chambersburg PA
CBHW021156160426
43194CB00007B/772